▼

Preaching Prophetically
When the News Disturbs

Preaching Prophetically When the News Disturbs

Interpreting the Media

AUDREY BORSCHEL

CHALICE
PRESS

ST. LOUIS, MISSOURI

Bible quotations, unless otherwise noted, are from the *New Revised Standard Version Bible,* copyright 1989, Division of Christian Education of the National Council of the Churches of Christ in the United States of America. Used by permission. All rights reserved.

Cover image: FotoSearch

Cover and interior design: Elizabeth Wright

Visit Chalice Press on the World Wide Web at
www.chalicepress.com

10   9   8   7   6   5   4   3   2   1   09   10   11   12   13   14

Library of Congress Cataloging-in-Publication Data
Borschel, Audrey.
 Preaching prophetically when the news disturbs : interpreting the media / Audrey Borschel.
    p. cm.
  ISBN 978-0-8272-3009-5
  1. Preaching. 2. Mass media–Religious aspects–Christianity. I. Title.

BV4211.3.B67 2009
251–dc22

2008044098

Printed in the United States of America

Contents

Foreword   vii

Acknowledgments   ix

Prayer for Preachers   x

Introduction   1

1. Preaching and the News That Disturbs   5

2. The News as Commerce   29

3. The Media Literacy Toolbox   49

4. Preacher as Mediator of the News and the Good News   73

5. What Preachers Can Learn from Journalists   103

6. Behind the Scenes of the First "Preaching When the News Disturbs" Workshop   117

Appendix A: The Roots of Today's Disturbing News and the Implications for Preaching   133

Appendix B: "Lament and Remember"   148

Appendix C: "If the Roof Is an Obstacle..."   152

Appendix D: Survey about News   156

Appendix E: "Stocking the Spiritual Pantry"   160

Appendix F: "National Day of Prayer and Remembrance"   164

Notes   167

Foreword

After thirty-nine years in the preaching ministry, my one lasting regret has to do with the ways I have succumbed to one or another of my congregations' unspoken contracts for silence. When in our families and congregations we convey a silent expectation not to mention or engage the hard.and disturbing stuff of life, we cut ourselves adrift from the cultural possibility and divine necessity of engaging the big questions, such as gender, sexuality, politics, ecology, faith, pluralism, and truth. We can give over all too readily to well-practiced social impulses to trivialize, polarize, demonize, or dominate. For all our loud hype and numbing verbosity, we can passively agree as families, congregations, or society to fall silent on what matters most. To the extent that our homes, congregations, public media, or assembly halls fall silent with respect to reverent curiosity and collaborative dialogue, we fail ourselves.

This social failure does not bode well for those of us called to be ministers of the Word. If we as Christians conspire with unspoken or spoken cultural impulses to marginalize or silence the most courageous and reflective voices among us, how are we to speak the Gospel? God is a living Word among us, inviting us at times to rewrite the social contracts of our public and private conversation. In this context, media literacy becomes an important steppingstone for pastors and people of faith as we journey intentionally on a path to informed reflection and renewed discourse on behalf of social action for the common good.

At a seminary staff meeting a few weeks ago, we were dealing with an imminent and somewhat unwelcome news story about local ecclesiastical affairs. I sarcastically remarked that I would like to visit a journalism school and ask just what reporters think they do—report the news or create it? A colleague, himself a former television and newspaper reporter, challenged my remark with what was in effect a call to more intentional media literacy.

These days, the church itself often is the protagonist in news that disturbs. Meanwhile, just like our listeners and our neighbors, we preachers can all too easily fall prey to the polarizing, accusatory, and silencing impulses of our disturbed, disturbing world. For those of us entrusted with the privilege of the pulpit, media literacy should be considered obligatory. The people of God deserve media-literate preachers, just as society deserves a media-literate church. For the sake of the Gospel, we as pastors are called by the urgent news of our times to learn the art of engaged, public reflection—to be informed about the news, to learn from our neighbors as we search reflectively for truth, to stay in touch with our feelings and know what is at stake, to walk humbly from inner authority informed by the Gospel, and to preach the reign of God. With these aspirations in mind, we pastors and preachers can ever-better proclaim the Good News that God is among us to disturb the unholy silences of our all-too-disturbing world.

I have read and studied this book with great benefit. Thank you, Audrey Borschel, for so capably volunteering to be our guide, as we—both pastors and parishioners—endeavor to understand the role and message of the media in terms of our Christian commitment to the Gospel, to the ministry of preaching, and to the world in which we live and serve.

Gregory Heille, O.P.
Aquinas Institute of Theology, St. Louis

Acknowledgments

This book would not have been completed without the gentle, but persistent prodding of my husband Mike Borschel and Professor Greg Heille, O.P. of Aquinas Institute of Theology. I am grateful to Mike for carefully reading and commenting on the manuscript at every stage and to Greg for his guidance from the inception of the project in 2003. As well, I benefited greatly from working with Dr. Richard Stern, who introduced me to the complex and fascinating world of media literacy.

I want to thank several of my colleagues in ministry who gave me valuable feedback after reading the manuscript: Rev. Duncan Macpherson, Jim Welter, Joe Zelenka, Rev. Verity Jones, Anne Hamilton, and Jim Hayes.

I have appreciated the encouragement of family and friends during the long process of writing.

Many thanks to listeners in many churches for the privilege of sharing the word with you and for your responses that have helped me grow and deepen my call to the preaching ministry.

My gratitude always to Chalice Press for having confidence in this project.

Thanks be to God, Author of life and hope, who is the Good News in the midst of the news that disturbs.

Prayer for Preachers

God of Hope,
Bless the preachers of the world with powerful,
indestructible faith.
Help them persevere as agents for change, troubling
and disturbing as the prophets of old.
May they embody peace, justice, and unconditional
love for all.
May your Spirit supply them with divine energy to heal
in your name until evil and suffering are defeated.
May your words be their words as they follow the
Eternal Word. Amen.

Introduction

As we approach the end of the first decade of the twentieth century, the themes of much disturbing news replay as variations on stories from the beginning of the new millennium. We were preoccupied with war in Afghanistan as well as in Iraq, the war on terrorism, and the spread of radical Islam. Oppression in Darfur, Sudan, a growing debate about global warming, corporate scandals, and lawsuits brought by victims molested by clergy occupied the minds of our congregations. To these we've added much more profound concern for climate change, world hunger and a significant downturn in the economy.

Perhaps you've had opportunities to incorporate some of these issues during your Sunday messages, helping your listeners understand their moral and ethical implications based on your interpretation of the Bible's teaching. However, many preachers may ignore issues raised in these and other disturbing news stories because they are unsure how to communicate their thoughts without straying into the sensitive area of politics and pulpit. That uncertainty continues to inhibit many preachers today.

Preaching within the context of real life situations is common for those of us who try to make our messages relevant to our listeners. In the 1920s theologian Karl Barth suggested that young theologians read both newspapers and the Bible, but they should base their interpretations on the scriptures. He held journalists in high esteem because of their importance in helping to form public opinion.[1] Imagine what he would say today about the increased importance and scope of the work of journalists, in this age of mass media.

In the United States and much of the western world, we have been blessed with the tremendous gifts of a free press and laws that protect our freedom of expression. A multitude of news media produce abundant information that informs and assists us with choices we make as citizens in a democracy. Consider how cable and satellite services have made it possible for electronic news media to expand the number of talk radio shows, televised newscasts, podcasts, weblogs, and Web sites.

But news reporting has also become more complicated with the proliferation of undocumented information circulating on the Internet and by an increase in bloggers who may or may not verify facts or adhere to the same ethics as professional journalists. In addition, and this is not necessarily negative, media corporations have the freedom to control the content of their newscasts and the way the news is presented based on their business plans and political perspectives. How can we become well-informed about the major stories as we sift through a daunting volume of material? How do we know when significant issues are under-reported or suppressed? We can accomplish this by becoming *media literate.*

Media literacy is a relatively new discipline. It developed when parents and educators raised concerns about violence, advertising content, perceived intolerance, and explicit sexuality in media, believing that the content of some media presentations may negatively influence children's behaviors. For many years, teachers have been incorporating lesson plans into their curricula to help children interpret media, so they can become better-informed consumers of the programming directed toward them.[2]

Preachers, too, can benefit from learning these same techniques, which were designed to evaluate media presentations for accuracy and objectivity. Media literacy tools help us confirm facts, distinguish editorial biases, and become aware of our own biases and perspectives.

When people are touched by local, national, or international news, they understandably bring their fears and concerns into worship. As pastoral preachers we have a unique responsibility to help our listeners place disturbing events in a Gospel context. We can accomplish this by immersing ourselves in the news stories that affect our listeners and by plumbing the Bible, as well as our community's sacramental tradition, for resources and rituals that will send our listeners forth from worship reassured by the Good News of faith.

This book seeks to help preachers interpret the news stories of our day by presenting information about the media industry that produces them. My objective and hope is that preachers will follow important news events closely, gather information from several sources, and interpret news presentations using the media literacy techniques presented in chapter 3. Then preachers will be prepared to achieve the second objective of this book, which is to address pastorally and courageously the theological, moral, and ethical issues presented in the news through the lens of the Gospel.

Chapter 1 establishes a biblical context for preaching the news that disturbs and discusses the role of the church and its preachers in civil society. I define what I consider to be disturbing news likely to shake the faith and well-being of the community and provide a brief background to the roots of the disturbing news, which is continued later in appendix A.

Chapter 2 describes the business of news presentations and how corporate news has evolved over the past few decades. Significant factors include business decisions by media owners that may affect newsgathering and distribution, government regulations, and how media professionals evaluate themselves and their industry.

Chapter 3 provides several media literacy tools that show how news stories are created, constructed, and presented. With this information, preachers will be able to "deconstruct" messages and weigh the merits of media presentations.

Chapter 4 develops a homiletical foundation for preaching when the news disturbs. It offers suggestions for preaching pastorally when interpreting the news in light of scripture by locating ingredients of consolation, hope, and resurrection in the news and the Good News.

Chapter 5 invites the discipline of journalism to inform preaching by examining the work of major opinion columnists who deal with some of the most pressing justice issues with which preachers and their listeners are also concerned.

Chapter 6 listens in on a workshop where participants were engaged with the concepts of the book. It offers ideas for hands-on activities and reflection questions to use in congregational forums or discussions with ordained and lay preachers. Included are a variety of experiences using different learning styles that cover the principles of media literacy and preaching pastorally when the news disturbs.

When preachers and listeners find it difficult to speak to or receive messages that take sides on controversial issues, the reasons are understandable. Disturbing news is more than print on newspaper or an image on the screen. It is often powerful enough to invade our emotional space, affect our daily decisions, and become part of our identity.

Too often, preachers and listeners have insufficient or inaccurate knowledge about the issues, or preachers fear reprisal from congregations that haven't been prepared to grapple boldly with the ethical and moral implications arising from disturbing news. Thus preachers choose to remain silent and their congregations remain unequipped to deal with the problem issues that haunt their daily viewing and reading hours.

However, preachers can prepare their listeners to deal with serious and perhaps divisive news by reinforcing biblical ethics and morality and making explicit connections to the troublesome issues that compose so much of the news.

Although some preachers do speak prophetically about events in the world around them, how effective have they been? A survey taken in 2003 showed that regarding contemporary major issues, media shaped 41 percent of the thinking of the American people, while religious beliefs influenced only 10 percent of those polled.[3] Media literate preachers should be able to bring these numbers into closer balance if we deal with issues that most concern our listeners and address them in light of the Gospel.

Realizing the significance of the challenge ahead of us, I dedicate this book to my preacher colleagues who persevere in applying the Gospel in difficult times and when confronted by the disturbing news of our world. May our preaching be prophetic, relevant, practical, and pastoral as we draw closer to the living Word of God in this troubled, earthly reign of God.

1

Preaching and the News
That Disturbs

NAZARETH–Members of the synagogue reacted in disbelief today after a local carpenter, Jesus, son of Mary and Joseph, read from the Isaiah scroll and claimed the scripture had been fulfilled in their hearing: "The Spirit of the Lord is upon me, because he has anointed me to bring good news to the poor. He has sent me to proclaim release to the captives and recovery of sight to the blind, to let the oppressed go free, to proclaim the year of the Lord's favor."[1] Enraged by his refusal to perform healings as he had done in neighboring towns, members of the local synagogue drove him out of Nazareth.

Preaching Biblical Justice

On that Sabbath morning, the listeners preferred entertainment in the form of healings and miracles to hearing more about Jesus' mission of teaching and preaching God's justice and love. Today's preachers of the Gospel have been ordained or called to share in this sacred obligation. To do this well, each of us will study the gospels to form a clear portrait of Jesus as preacher, teacher, and activist and discover how we identify with him. Just as Jesus responded to some of the critical issues of his day, we will also, if we choose to preach biblical justice and make the scriptural texts come alive in our communities of faith. To provide insights into the particularly difficult issues that affect us and our listeners, we will add a variety of media resources to our dialogue with scripture and our theological tradition.

Let me begin, then, by reflecting on my perception of Jesus and his ministry. Here are some of my thoughts from an essay I wrote on preaching, which I hope will inspire you to add your own:

> God chose to communicate with us through the humanity of Jesus. The Jesus with whom I identify my life and ministry, was fully human, passionate, relational, and totally self-giving. Jesus, the enfleshment of God, offered a unique path toward holiness, providing redemption to a religious society that needed transforming. I admire the simplicity and humility with which he presented his messages of love and the preferential option for the poor, but I hear a dialectical voice that decries how this message has been diluted and filtered over centuries of political and ecclesial accretions and detours from the path.
>
> The Jesus who speaks to me from the Gospels and who preaches to my community is a risk-taking dissenter, neither passive nor *nice* much of the time. If I preach this Word who speaks to my heart, I must reflect his passionate, countercultural, and radical character. When Jesus identified and preached against injustice, he irritated complacent and advantaged people. Our culture today continues to resist revising attitudes and policies that would favor the poor and oppressed. The *not-yet* illusiveness of the Reign of God prods me to preach against complacency and for our ongoing conversion.[2]

Should we choose to follow the path of Jesus as preacher and teacher, who lived fully within his time and culture, we are obliged to question and comment on the ethics and morality of issues in the news. Sometimes that means challenging policies, statements, and acts by people in government, as well as corporate leaders or other public figures who exert influence. Although it would be easier for us to remain silent, we need only recall what happened as Germany's Third Reich gained momentum. Many preachers in German churches failed to speak out, and so they effectively became agents/pastors for the Nazi regime. Might the outcome have been different if more preachers had courageously spoken out against Nazi doctrines, teaching their congregations how these policies were incompatible with the teachings of Jesus? Are we capable of protesting or resisting in our time should we believe that unethical, immoral, or unjust actions are being perpetrated in our own country—or are we too timid? Consider how these words from a mid-1980s National Council of Churches newsletter in the Philippines apply to us today:

> To interpret the Word of God in a sermon means making the Word of God *bear upon* a specific problem, a particular situation, a concrete issue, a definite life situation. The Word of God is nothing unless it strikes people in their lives, their communities, institutions, cultures, and their destinies. And it strikes them in judgment, mercy, and promise, aiming at *change* (repentance) to bring about more love, more justice, more truth, more freedom, more peace, and more praises of God in human life and affairs.
>
> If, therefore, the Word of God is properly interpreted in a sermon, a preacher may have to draw out specific implications and conclusions that indicate the significance of God's Word for now, for today, in our contemporary life situation. And the implication or conclusion should be critical of current trends, prevailing situations, etc.[3]

The Nature of Disturbing News

Negative news disturbs us in different ways, depending on our experiences, interests, and familiarity with the issues. I hope preacher colleagues will agree that news is disturbing when the details conflict with the moral and ethical teachings of Jesus. I define disturbing news as those events and issues that are violent, unjust, destabilizing, inhumane, uncharitable, and all policies and actions that will harm the environment. In addition, I include acute crises, such as natural disasters and accidents, and chronic worldwide social and political challenges for which solutions are few, slow, and inadequate. Disturbing news impacts us whether it originates locally or globally. Some of us may be more disturbed by news that affects us personally, such as the closing of a plant where family members have worked, or by the sudden death of a beloved friend or local leader, although crises that emerge on the national or world stage often move us to weep, reflect, pray, and take action.

Looking back over the early years of the twenty-first century, we have experienced all manner of disturbing news events, but I would rank the terrorist attacks on the World Trade Center and the Pentagon on September 11, 2001, as the event with the most impact. Javier Navia, writing in *La Nación,* summed it up very powerfully:

History has recorded many turning points–events that on account of their political or social magnitude have changed the world, marking the end of one era and the beginning of another.... But very few times, perhaps never as on Sept. 11, 2001, have these events occurred in a matter of seconds, in the time it took a Boeing to slice through a steel and glass building and touch off a conflagration capable of bringing down one of the greatest structures ever erected by humans, while the whole planet looked on live and direct in speechless horror. Only one thing was certain: Something had changed forever.... It is difficult to remember the events that were news this year, because what happened before Sept. 11 seems so far away in time.[4]

While isolated terrorist attacks had been carried out abroad and had garnered significant media coverage, the first attacks on U.S. soil were accompanied by a surge in media coverage that raised public awareness about the phenomenon of a resurgence of a militant, radical form of Islam, based on Wahhabi theology, a movement begun in the eighteenth century to purify Islam on the Arabian peninsula. (For additional background information on radical Islam, as well as on the historical and sociological roots of much of today's news, see appendix A.)

All news media were saturated with information about Islam and radical jihadists who are determined to destroy the Western way of life. Disturbing news about ongoing terrorist threats continues to occupy media, keeping fear of more attacks alive and influencing the course of politics, including public policy and legislation in several countries.[5] We have seen how a single disturbing news event can leave long lasting repercussions. The disturbing events of 9/11 ushered in a protracted era of combat, begun when particular government leaders inaccurately linked the terrorist attacks to Saddam Hussein, dictator of Iraq.

The violent chain of events that led to the destruction of the Iraqis' way of life has involved hundreds of thousands of U.S. military and civilian personnel assigned to duty in Iraq, with many of the military personnel serving multiple tours in the combat zone while spouses and children suffer family upheaval because of their absence. Not inconsequential are 4,195 confirmed American military deaths by mid-November 2008. An under-reported Rand Corporation study released on April 18, 2008 revealed that 300,000 veterans of wars in Iraq and Afghanistan have mental problems and that 320,000 have had brain injuries.[6]

Years after the attacks on the U.S., Middle East stability remains threatened by the spread of the radical Islamists' movement in Asia and Africa. The Israel-Palestine peace negotiations and a two-state political solution remain in jeopardy. At this writing, the political futures of Afghanistan and Pakistan are uncertain, especially as the Taliban appear to be gaining strength and influence.

In his column for Memorial Day 2008, George Will illustrated how another single incident changed the course of history and how it is connected to our current world situation.

On June 28, 1914, an assassin's bullet in Sarajevo killed the heir to the throne of the Austro-Hungarian empire. The war that followed took more than 116,000 American lives—more than all of America's wars after the Second World War. And in a sense, the First World War took many more American lives because it led to the Second World War and beyond.

The First World War is still taking American lives because it destroyed the Austro-Hungarian, Romanoff and Ottoman empires. A shard of the latter is called Iraq.[7]

Many of today's major media stories chronicle ongoing centuries-old struggles, such as human rights violations, where ethnic groups continue to show vast contempt for the value of human life, such as those who perpetrate genocide and starvation against the people of Darfur, Sudan, and Somalia, as well as the exploitation and debasement of other ethnic peoples. Violence in South Africa has increased against immigrants from Zimbabwe who came there to escape deplorable economic conditions and food shortages.[8] Reports from Asia reveal a vast sex slave industry in the midst of a boom in manufacturing activity.

In the United States, ongoing yet urgent disturbing issues exacerbated by the financial crisis require attention and policy reform—dealing with serious crime in our cities; providing social services, including health care and insurance, food, and employment for our poor; improving the quality of care in our nursing homes; addressing the early needs of children and parents to prepare them for learning. While a large number of our citizens have experienced massive corporate layoffs and outsourcing, top executives have received unprecedented benefits. Local plant closings cause local economies in the surrounding area to suffer, as well as the workers.

High gasoline prices and major increases in food costs, plus the economic slump finally officially called a recession, became disturbing news to many Americans in 2008. The crisis in the sub-prime mortgage market plunged many homeowners into foreclosure.[9] New housing and other construction slowed dramatically, forcing layoffs throughout the construction industry.[10]

Many Americans vent their frustrations about the disturbing news by blaming undocumented workers for the woes of the country. While the immigration issue has been mired in the special interests of politicians and business leaders for decades, no amount of legislative energy has been able to produce a workable and humane compromise. Of major concern to preachers is that amid the fears of terrorism and economic challenges our listeners may join the growing numbers of people who are expressing their intolerance of newcomers, especially Muslims and Latinos. How can we respond to such enormous challenges through our witness as Christians, especially as preachers of the Gospel? On the other hand, how can we justify *not* addressing these vital issues that touch so many people within God's realm?

Illegal immigration is disturbing news to many people. It is an issue that concerns citizens in countries all over the world, as noted earlier when mentioning violence against Zimbabwean immigrants in South Africa. In the United States, some people are concerned that undocumented immigrants take jobs away from others, or that they usurp educational and health services. Other Americans are concerned that employers exploit undocumented workers by underpaying them and forcing them to work long hours, also that arrests of workers at factories by federal authorities and subsequent deportations create hardships for children who may become separated from their parents.

Many disturbing events challenge us and our listeners. Preachers who choose to help their listeners understand how faith intersects with life will study the issues, intentionally gathering information from various media sources to gain a fuller picture than what we can understand from meager "briefs" or sound bites that alert us to disturbing news but often fall short of providing adequate information. Such superficial coverage limits our ability to understand complex issues. In subsequent chapters we'll discover why we must consult different media to gain the widest perspective on the story.

Here are a few of the reasons. Editorial decisions regarding which stories we see and hear and how they are told is one factor in how much comprehensive news we receive. Another is the tendency for media outlets to position stories on the page or during a newscast based on perception of consumer interest. Even censorship comes into play as media executives decide who among candidates will receive interviews.[11] A troubling trend is that lifestyle and entertainment stories compete with hard-core news, often taking more space or airtime than items we should learn about in detail. Preachers will not try to discuss all the news that disturbs during Sunday preaching. But on many occasions we can make connections between troubling current issues and the biblical passages on which we preach. What better opportunities do we have than the weekends when we celebrate civic holidays, such as Memorial Day, Independence Day, or Veterans Day to promote the non-violent message of Jesus? For example, I knew my congregation would expect me to incorporate Memorial Day, but I hoped that if I stressed the significance of honoring the fallen that they would be receptive to the higher value of peacemaking over waging war. This sermon from May 25, 2008, may be found in appendix B.

Preaching and the First Amendment to the Constitution

If you've preached against a policy or a piece of legislation, has a listener ever accosted you and complained that you violated the Constitution's doctrine of separation of church and state? All preachers should understand that no legal restrictions prevent preachers from presenting conclusions from the scriptures and Christian tradition that may be critical of actions taken or contemplated by the government.

The First Amendment to the Constitution of the United States reads: "Congress shall make no law respecting an establishment of religion, or prohibiting the free exercise thereof..." A common understanding of that clause regarding the separation of church and state is that the government may not establish an official religion or force citizens to accept particular religious doctrine, nor may it limit people from practicing their religion. Preachers are, however, legally responsible for adhering to the regulations stated in the Internal Revenue Code. Since churches and charities are tax-exempt under the Internal Revenue Code, they pay no federal taxes as long as they conform to its regulations. In 1954 that code was amended to impose limits on political activity by not-for-profits and churches. The revised rules stipulated that clergy, speaking on behalf of their congregations, may preach about moral or political issues as long as they don't endorse or speak against candidates. Preachers may not interfere with their listeners' freedom to choose their elected leaders. Otherwise, preachers may interpret the Bible as they see fit. That means all preachers have the freedom to deliver messages on all the concerns of our people, from what we believe God wants us to do for the poor to how we feel about policies or legislation. Clergy are also free to express their personal political views as long as they clearly delineate these views as their own and not those of the church.[12]

You've heard it said that pulpit and politics don't mix, but we need to clarify what we mean by the term "politics." Defining it narrowly, some Americans think of politics as what occurs during election campaigns, confining its meaning to government matters. But James Madison more broadly considered politics a study of human nature, which covers a wide swath of activities in the world.[13] Politics has to do with power—how it's assumed or shared, how certain rules or concepts form group and individual behavior, how these ideas are decided and implemented. Not only is the term "politics" defined as "the art or science of government," but also as "the total complex of relations between those living in society."[14] In this sense, religious institutions are political, for they, too, establish rules or codes for their adherents. They are affected by changes in the nation's laws, and they lobby lawmakers to implement or retract legislation.

Clearly religious pluralism tests the political power of traditional religious institutions, adding new ideas about faith and theology to our religious landscape. Some religious groups amass large blocs of sectarian voters who contribute vast sums to voice their approval or disapproval of policies and elections. Certain groups focus on wedge issues such as abortion and same-sex marriage, while others gather public support by lobbying for increased services to help the poor, including improved healthcare coverage and a living wage, for example, as their way of making the Gospel of Jesus real in their time.

Jesus and Politics

Political tensions between the Romans and Jews were held in check during the Roman occupation of Palestine because Roman authorities placed Jewish client kings who were subservient to Rome over local affairs. During the years of Jesus' public ministry, Herod Antipas ruled the areas of the Galilee and Perea, while Pontius Pilate governed in Judea. As long as they cooperated with the Romans, the Sadducees, (the Jerusalem Temple's High Priests), remained in control of political and religious power in Jerusalem. The gospels report that Jesus preached against some of the traditional interpretations of Torah, especially as they affected the social policies of the religious institution. Was his teaching political when he spoke truth to power, despite the fact that none of the gospel writers connected Jesus with a particular branch of Judaism or with a political movement?

Jesus voiced his dissatisfaction with both the Sadducees and Pharisees for their narrow interpretations of Torah, particularly for excluding or discriminating against the anawim, the impoverished, those who most need God's help. According to the gospels he never sought political power. In John 6:15–16, not only did he deny aspirations to be a king, but he escaped from those who wanted to effect his coronation. However, he spoke of a "kingdom of God" as a power structure in which God calls everyone to radical spiritual conversion through their practice of justice and love for all. After John the Baptist affirmed him as the new leader of this movement for change, Jesus developed a power base among simple fishermen. Soon additional supporters came on board, and some of these sustained the movement by providing material help. Jesus never advocated overthrowing the Roman government by force. He worked from within the structure of Judaism to change the behavior of its leaders and adherents. The kingdom he preached was not of this world–rather it was situated within the world, but transcended it. This inclusive realm of God stretched beyond all political and social boundaries, beyond concrete geographic places and ultimately beyond any specific religious group. Jesus set out to build this realm by making a mission statement out of the Isaiah text he appropriated at the Nazareth synagogue. The completion of this kingdom would not be limited by time or place, for it was (and is) in process. "To seek the kingdom of God never meant anything less than to seek God's promised rule in the whole of reality, in space and time. Everything is included. Everyone is included."[15]

The work of Jesus' ministry cannot be separated from how Roman imperialism affected life for peasants in both Jerusalem and Galilee, nor can it be understood without knowing that frequent popular uprisings protested against the occupiers both before and after Jesus.

> It is not surprising that popular protest and resistance erupted with increasing frequency precisely during the lifetime of Jesus and his followers. The popular messianic movements in Galilee and Judea attempted to establish the people's independence of both Jerusalem and Roman rule. Radical Pharisees and other teachers spearheaded a refusal to render the Roman tribute, claiming that God was their true and only Lord and Master. Popular prophets led movements anticipating, among other things, the collapse of high-priestly and Roman rule in Jerusalem, along with the walls of the city.[16]

In light of the undercurrent of unrest, an emphasis on inclusion as a distinguishing mark of the kingdom becomes more understandable in the gospel accounts of Jesus' countercultural relationships. These familiar examples reveal how Jesus shared his vision of God's kingdom, by including those who were considered unworthy by the religious establishment. Jesus ate with society's outcasts, such as the tax collector Levi and others (Lk. 5:27–32; Lk.15:1–7; Lk.19:1–10). He included foreigners, telling the story of the Samaritan man who took a Jewish man left to die in a ditch to an inn even as his own religious people passed him by (Lk.10:25–37), and even healed Gentiles (Mk.7:24–30; Mt.7:5–13). Jesus fed the hungry and performed healings even on the Sabbath (Mt.12:1–8; Lk.13:10–17). He angered the religious leaders by throwing those engaged in commerce out of the Temple courtyard to keep the place of prayer holy (Mk.11:15–17; Lk.19:45–46). Jesus preached justice and mercy in the Sermon on the Mount, identifying the kingdom as the locus for doing God's will. The kingdom brings caring both on earth and in heaven for all the blessed, the suffering, grieving, thirsting, persecuted, peacemakers, and all those who are powerless, including the women and children of his time (Mt. 5–7). And the seat of the kingdom's power was to be within us, where we are guided by divine presence.

Our World and Political Preaching

Like the world of Jesus and of the first disciples, our world is a violent place, with poor and oppressed people all around us, with special interests of some powerful people trumping the welfare of others. Are people better off since Jesus began to enact his vision of God's realm? Have churches, the organized heirs of this vision, responded vigorously enough to Jesus' plan for building the kingdom by extending the realm to encompass everyone? Preachers are uniquely positioned to lead their congregations toward welcoming and building the realm of God by connecting the Gospel with disturbing news and meeting God's people in their pain. As Australian theologian William Loader reflects:

> The poor are by and large poor, the hungry still hungry, the weeping still weeping, the life and love of God still spurned and rejected. We rarely pause to face this reality. And yet facing the reality of such pain is a creative moment. It enables us to listen to what is happening in the world around us, and to listen to what is happening inside ourselves. Our temptation will always be to avoid pain, to deny that it is there, to explain it, to compensate for it. I believe it to be one of the most important events in the Christian pilgrimage. Because it is a

point of pain it is a centre of enormous energy…. It can also be a major step together on Christ's way.[17]

Preaching about the news that disturbs can be political in the same sense as Jesus' mission was political. The news that disturbed Jesus brought to light the injustice of exclusion, the degradation of human beings by political and religious systems that failed to celebrate that all people are made in God's image. *However, activist preaching is not the same as politicizing religion.* Politicization of religion in the U.S. occurs when individuals or groups insist that their religious beliefs require that certain laws be adopted, that specific candidates be elected who endorse their views, or that sectarian prayer be employed to open government meetings as a political tool to maintain the image of America as a Christian nation. Ideally, the followers of Jesus in a pluralistic society seek to include all people and work together to implement an umbrella of loving practices, as he taught us to do.

Understanding the Civil Religion of the United States and Its Influence

The founders of the newly formed United States of America were adamant that the government would show no preference for one religion over another. This was in response to the practices of European theocracies that integrated the tenets of the official religion into government as well as private life, often causing great suffering to those with different beliefs. That didn't mean, however, that the United States would eliminate all references to God in public speech, on buildings, or on coinage. Nor would prayer be forbidden before meetings where public policy was made. However, some of the representatives to the first Continental Congress were uncomfortable with the idea of praying with their colleagues because they were a group of diverse believers, including Episcopalians, Quakers, Anabaptists, Congregationalists, and even simple theists. Some objected to having a prayer delivered by a Church of England clergyman because of his ties to the Crown. Others were open to all prayers devoutly offered.

Since 1774 when representatives to the Continental Congress debated about opening their session with prayer, the number of religious traditions practiced in America has expanded exponentially. Numerous Christian denominations emerged on the American frontier, and a variety of Christian, Jewish, Muslim, Buddhist, Hindu, Native American, and other worship traditions brought by immigrants or created here enriched our cultural and religious landscape.[18]

However, with religious pluralism, the type and even the use of religious language in public discourse by government officials and clergy has raised issues of appropriateness with many more citizens identifying with religions not based on Judeo-Christian scripture and tradition. Traditionally, presidential addresses have made inclusive references to God, avoiding sectarian or biblical language. However, in recent years, presidential and other patriotic addresses have introduced a distinctly Christian tone, with quotes from the New Testament, and this has raised some questions about what constitutes "civil" religion.

One of my colleagues, Rev. James Wolfe, defines civil religion as "devotion to a nation and its leaders, its ideals and gods, as expressed in words, such as speeches, songs, and documents, and deeds, such as ceremonies, wars and monuments."[19] Writing during the civil rights era, Robert Bellah observed:

> Behind the civil religion at every point lie biblical archetypes: Exodus, Chosen People, Promised Land, New Jerusalem, and Sacrificial Death and Rebirth. But it is also genuinely American and genuinely new. It has its own prophets and its own martyrs, its own sacred events and sacred places, its own solemn rituals and symbols. It is concerned that America be a society as perfectly in accord with the will of God as men can make it, and a light to all nations.[20]

Years ago, a particular understanding of the meaning of separation of church and state led to an unspoken social contract in the United States that kept many preachers from criticizing the positions taken by the government in exchange for the government's relative "hands-off" policy regarding the business of the church. Roderick P. Hart discussed this phenomenon in *The Political Pulpit*.[21] In 2002, the Religious Communication Association devoted a special issue of its publication, *The Journal of Communication and Religion*,[22] to reflections on Hart's earlier work, with Hart himself contributing the concluding essay.

The journal presented significant insights about civil religion and its relationship to sectarian religion. Some of the contributors described how patriotism can evolve into civil religion:

- when the President of the United States invokes God in his speeches
- when religious services or observances are held under the auspices of the government

- when the flag is revered as an icon representing the ideals of the nation
- when policies are implemented that require the treasure and sacrifice of its citizens, as well as their allegiance

In these examples, the government can become a powerful religious force in the land, even when there is a careful absence of denominationalism in the rhetoric or when no legislation is enacted. Churches often absorb civil religion into their worship, incorporating flags and patriotism. Sometimes the media blur the lines between patriotism and religion and exacerbate the tension inherent in civil religion when they report on patriotic speeches where speakers have expressed their religious values in the midst of discussing affairs of the secular state.[23] This conflation can confuse and even alarm some Americans who respect cultural and religious diversity, as well as separation of church and state. In addition, the media have exploited religion during high profile campaigns as candidates submit to being quizzed on their religious beliefs and practices while the public learns less about the their positions on domestic and foreign policies.

For example, during the early stages of the 2008 presidential primaries and caucuses, the strong religious beliefs of two Republican candidates, Mormon Mitt Romney and former Baptist minister Mike Huckabee, dominated political news stories. Ruben Navarette of the *San Diego Union-Tribune* commented on how media were overreaching by framing religious issues in the campaign to create divisiveness in society.[24] By April 2008, the controversial preaching of Barack Obama's former pastor, Rev. Jeremiah Wright, eclipsed all policy issues as inflammatory sound bites from his sermons were replayed over and over, creating a diversion for voters and a public relations crisis for Sen. Obama.[25] Always alert to the prospect of controversial issues, the media observe and explore palpable tensions in the country concerning religion. Here are some important questions that will continue to affect both preachers and listeners in our society:

- How does a political leader with deep religious convictions live his/her faith publicly, while not imposing those religious beliefs on public policy?
- Will some Christian groups continue to resist accepting religious pluralism as a fact in the U.S. or become more tolerant and less vocal about the supremacy of their beliefs?
- How will political leaders resolve the issues of mixing patriotic and religious language in our pluralistic society, as well as the form prayer should assume in public places?

- Will religious tests be banned for elections or political appointments?
- How do pastors and preachers navigate the minefield of civil religion, when listeners are accustomed to mixing religious faith and patriotism?

An advocate of religious pluralism, Reverend C. Welton Gaddy, president of the Interfaith Alliance Foundation, once remarked:

> The President of the United States is the political leader of the nation, not the religious leader. Just as religion should not be a test for any political candidate for public office, religion should not be a tool of any political leader in a public office. In no way should the President of the United States politicize religion or by the use of religious language from one particular religious tradition alienate citizens from other traditions or no tradition... [26]

Gaddy also noted that while civil religion has always been an underpinning of patriotism, the religious language of Evangelical Christianity, which began to be heard in political speeches from 2000, excluded many people who don't understand, identify with, or agree with the content.[27] The picture has been changing over the last few years, with the voices representing the moderate evangelical Christian movement, such as Rev. Jim Wallis, becoming more prominent as the influence of fundamentalist Christian leaders recedes. A theological statement released by several Evangelical leaders on May 7, 2008, *An Evangelical Manifesto*, reveals a new emphasis on social justice and environmental concerns, as well as a strong condemnation of using Christian beliefs as "weapons for political interests."[28] In contrast with the early part of the decade, the rhetoric of new national leaders avoids sectarian references.

One of the reasons that civil religion is prominent is that television, radio, and the Internet present presidential speeches in real time as news, while leaders of sectarian churches lack similar access and resources to respond and to provide balance for the comments by government leaders. Accordingly, Hart describes the influence of the churches as mainly rhetorical, while the civil government's influence is global and carries the authority of law. Which group has more influence, then, the government, with its immediate access to media, or the churches, whose preached messages reach less than half the population?

The influence of civil religion was apparent during the buildup to the Iraq War. Numerous reporters and editorial writers in major and smaller markets criticized the president's use of religious language. An editorial in the March 8, 2003, issue of the mainstream Protestant weekly, *The Christian Century*, observed "The president's faith is shaping his public policies," and remarked, "What is alarming is that Bush seems to have no reservations about the notion that God and the good are squarely on the American side."[29]

While leaders of national organizations representing mainline Protestants and Catholics attempted to persuade the Bush administration to adopt a policy of restraint before going to war with Iraq, these dissenters from the administration's position were ineffective when they offered "Just War" or other moral arguments. Many preachers, including myself, preached restraint, hoping our listeners would also try to influence the course of events. My sermon from that liminal time is included in appendix C. However, the popular civil religion in 2003, characterized by a conflation of religious identity with unquestionable patriotism, strongly influenced by conservative Christian groups that supported the war policy, some even justifying it on religious grounds.[30]

Martin J. Medhurst, a contributor to *The Journal of Communication and Religion*'s special issue on civil religion, felt that Hart should have noticed the rise of organizations promoting the views of the Religious Right in the 1970s, prior to Ronald Reagan's presidency:

> He was on the cusp of a major revolution in religion-government relations. Indeed, the revolution had already begun, but neither its existence nor its implications were acknowledged in the book. According to Hart the "contract" between the parties was this: religion agrees to stay out of electoral politics and governance in exchange for the right to display the rhetoric of civil piety on ritualized occasions of state such as inaugurations, Fourth of July celebrations, bicentennial events, presidential prayer breakfasts, and the like. Religion's role is symbolic and rhetorical only, and when it dares to speak its name outside of these carefully circumscribed boundaries, it is to be met with disdain, umbrage, and ultimately, rejection... Between the time that Hart issued his book and today, we've had the Religious Roundtable, The Christian Voice, The Moral Majority, Concerned Women for America, the American Family

Association, the Family Research Council, and, of course, the Christian Coalition.[31]

As Medhurst noted, organized religion had expanded far beyond congregations of established denominations to include faith-based agencies formed to lobby for political change. Today these draw from a broader base than individual churches and are often progressive and mission-focused rather than conservative, such as the ones mentioned in the quote above. Among them are two Catholic groups based in Washington, D.C., the international peace organization, Pax Christi, and the social-justice lobbying group, Network. Bread for the World, Heifer International, Habitat for Humanity, and the moderate evangelical Sojourners group are examples of ecumenical faith-based organizations working toward social change.

But, these organizations have not replaced local churches and their pastors, to whom people still turn for spiritual guidance. Church leaders in the United States, according to Hart's "contract," are not supposed to meddle in the politics of the civil religion, the sphere of the governing party. However, just as the ideas marking the boundaries of institutional religion and civil religion became blurred, so, too, were the legal markers, making official clarification necessary for politicians and clergy.

While preachers and congregations are prohibited from endorsing candidates, they may speak out against injustice, which includes questioning government policies when they contradict the Gospel. But before speaking out, preachers, as well as their listeners, will benefit from more information about the factors that influence media coverage of disturbing news regarding controversial government policies. When we know that a policy is morally wrong and potentially harmful, Hart's silent contract must be abrogated, and preachers must speak out. Hart's silent contract is abrogated whenever government or religious institutions overstep their boundaries by acting against the interests of the poor and oppressed, when they infringe on the rights of all citizens to their freedom of belief and religious practice, when they fail to respect religious pluralism, or when they interfere with the right of citizens to elect representatives.

Freedom Struggles and Liberation Theologies

Much of our world's disturbing news is rooted in unresolved, centuries-old freedom struggles. Chances are that you, someone you know, or one of your ancestors emigrated from another country to seek freedom from adverse political, religious, racial, or economic conditions. The memory remains in the people as they blame their current conditions on patronizing, former colonial rule, abuses of political power, and ethnic or religious intolerance. As we were reminded earlier in this chapter, history and geography provide many of the answers to the origins of today's disturbing situations.

While news media frequently cover world wide human struggles against oppression and injustice, media consumers often require repetitive exposure to news accounts, as well as in-depth, succinct coverage, to move from complacency to action.

For example, although the crisis in Darfur had been in the news for years, when I read a particular column by a political science professor, I finally understood more about this horrific situation.[32]

In various times and places, oppressed people have found hope and empowerment by studying their sacred scriptures and strengthening their resolve through prayer and reflection, often gaining courage to determine a course of action toward freedom from oppression. While the methods may vary, the process of study, prayer, and listening to God's leading forms the basis for "liberation theology." Liberation theology claims that God sides with the poor and oppressed against the oppressors. As Tony Campolo pointed out when he attempted to help the public understand the preaching of Rev. Jeremiah Wright (who comes out of a formation in black liberation theology, as well as a men's liberation theology), there are many nuances to liberation theology that serve gender, racial, ethnic and political needs.[33]

In terms of Christian faith and theology, liberation theologians seek hope and direction from within the tradition while keeping institutional and structural evil in tension. Liberation theologies evolve when people of faith try to overcome oppressive structures that have been responsible for marginalizing, limiting, neglecting, or annihilating their people. Over the past five hundred years, liberation theologies have become effective strategies for the poor who are trying to improve their living conditions in countries formerly governed by colonial powers that are now often led by dictators. For marginalized people, a theology of liberation can be a positive response to understand, reclaim, and even celebrate religious tradition in the context of mistreatment.

Preachers familiar with the Bible's narratives of the struggles for freedom within salvation history can relate them to accounts of more recent suffering. Christian liberation theologians and their supporters believe that the biblical accounts about the pursuit of freedom reveal a God who wants people to be free from control and domination by political leaders and institutions. Familiar examples are the exodus of the Israelites from slavery in Egypt, Queen Esther's advocacy for the Jews' safety in Persia, and the return of the Jews to Judea following the Babylonian captivity, or even Matthew's gospel with its imagery of Jesus as the new Moses. Liberation theology assists oppressed persons to recognize God's liberating power and particular love for the poor, enabling people who are deprived of freedom to develop hope for the future.

Liberation Theology as a Theology of Restoring Dignity to the "Other"

Whenever Jesus served suffering people, he also restored their dignity. He did the opposite of what oppressors usually do through economics, politics, military measures, and media. They control the lives of those they stigmatize as different, the nameless and faceless "others."[34] As liberation theologies develop among oppressed people, these "others" regain their names, dignity, and hope, even when the conditions that move them to reclaim their humanity change slowly, if at all. Resistance, as part of the praxis of liberation theologies, becomes successful when people choose to work in solidarity with one another, both by refusing to give up their cause and by believing in God's preference and love for the poor. Liberation theologies help people maintain hope where many would lose faith altogether. When preachers support the poor they are acting to make the Isaiah text that Jesus proclaimed in the Nazareth synagogue real in their time. Appendix A provides helpful insights about how disturbing news is related to major freedom movements, the politics of exclusion, the downside of globalization, and how religion and spirituality have empowered oppressed people into action through theological reflection.

Do You Agree with What Some Preachers and Listeners Think?

When I began to wrestle with the topic of preaching when the news disturbs, I developed a survey to test my thesis that preachers need to respond to disturbing news events by addressing them from the pulpit. Forty-five preachers, seminarians, and listeners from several states participated. Participants were asked which media they consulted for their news and how frequently they turned to their news sources. Other questions asked whether participants had been disturbed by news, what news disturbed them, how they identified critical issues in the news that deal with human struggle, what their experience had been of listening to preaching when news was disturbing, and their expectations for preaching in crisis situations. Respondents also were asked to indicate areas of knowledge they felt their preacher should possess.

I discovered that most of the total participants followed the news on television, then radio, newspaper, and the Internet. Most consulted their news sources several times a day. Word of mouth was the least frequent source for receiving news. In contrast, the "listeners" responded that they receive their news primarily from newspapers and television, but they consulted Internet news services more frequently than the ministers and seminarians. All but four individuals said they had been "disturbed, shocked, or frightened" by a news story, with the listeners indicating they were more disturbed by news of national or international concerns.

When asked which news issues on a list were particularly disturbing, most frequently checked were liberation struggles, domestic violence, war, terrorism in the United States and abroad, injustice toward individuals, and globalization. Write-in concerns included destruction of historical/cultural icons, violence in the name of religion, destruction of native habitats, racism, sexism, child molestation, rape, murder, serial killers, abduction, and snipers.[35]

A group of Catholic priests who responded to the survey placed injustice, poverty, terrorism, and issues regarding family members as their highest priority, writing in acts of injustice or violence involving children, stories about cruelty, bioethical issues, unrest in the Middle East, anti-life legislation, injustice in the church.

I asked the participants to name issues in the news that are rooted in human struggle and to describe the struggle and its causes. They named hate groups in Indiana, ethnic cleansing abroad, homelessness, Israeli-Palestinian struggle, economic embargo of Cuba, Afghanistan, Serbia, Pakistan-India, Missouri River control, Louisiana Wetland vs. Energy Corporation, disputes over fishing in Chesapeake Bay, civil rights struggle in the United States, female genital mutilation, clergy sexual abuse, and violence to children. Most of the people named the Israeli-Palestinian conflict.

Others listed ethnic cleansing, youth in China, illegal immigrants, apartheid, Afghanistan and Russia, North and South Korea, Rwandans and Tutus, indigenous people in Mexico, oppression of Iraqi people, the Chechnya/Russia conflict, Mexicans dying trying to come to the United States, 9/11, women's rights and domestic violence issues, and local poverty in the United States.

The listener group added sexual abuse by clergy and its cover-up, male dominance, greed, religious fanaticism, AIDS in Africa, the Israeli-Palestinian conflict as a struggle for place, potential attack on Iraq as a struggle for United States freedom in using lots of oil, the freedom to research and apply new information in genetics, subjugation of women in Third World countries, South Africa's move from apartheid to universal suffrage, and Civil Rights and the struggle for racial justice in the United States. Clearly, the people who responded understood how liberation struggles and theology are linked with justice issues in the news.

When I asked whether preachers should deal with disturbing news events from the pulpit, all but one replied "yes." Here are some of their eloquent comments:

- "If issues are not addressed from the pulpit, how will we ever deal with such news in a healthy, Christian manner?"
- "Qualified yes. We should be made aware of situations as they relate to issues involving human rights. It is not appropriate to seek validation or acceptance of a problem, nor is it acceptable to impose the values of some people on the entire congregation."
- "Preachers need to help people come to terms with what disturbs them, but not add to their anxiety merely to drive home some point a preacher might want to make."
- "Put in context of religious teaching and belief."
- "I believe that the scriptures have a lot to say to some of the issues in our world. Without 'sugar-coating' the hard realities, I believe that we must preach the hope we have as Christians in the face of the sins in our lives and of our world."
- "I feel that we are called to comment on the world, local, and societal events that impact our ability as Christians to truly live the Gospel message."
- "How can we not [deal with disturbing news form the pulpit]? Of course our focus must be the Gospel, not the news, but we must stay grounded in our experience of the world today."
- "I believe that preachers should address disturbing news from the pulpit. Ignoring the issues creates a sense among the listeners that the preacher is not in touch with current events, life situations, or problems in our society."
- "If our responsibility is to preach contextually, then disturbing news events cannot be ignored. A present example would be the Iraq situation."
- "Preachers should address disturbing news. It is on the minds of most members of the assembly anyway. I believe many people come expecting to hear these issues acknowledged in some

way. However the temptation which must be avoided is for the preacher to offer ready solutions to very complex problems."

- "We can help people connect with the struggles of others or help name how the disturbing news may be affecting them in the context of their faith and the Gospel."
- "These events touch our lives, either directly or tangentially, and beg for the light of the Gospel to be shown on them. To ignore the issues would be to suggest that the Gospel has nothing to offer in times of strife."

I asked whether they ever attended a service where the preacher failed to incorporate the news that disturbed in the preaching. Some said they were guilty of this themselves, and several replied that they rarely hear anyone else preach besides themselves. Here are some responses from active ministers:

- "I researched how different parishes dealt with 9/11 and was greatly saddened by a number of the responses."
- "It is disappointing not to hear a contextual approach to the homily, particularly if the news event is on everyone's mind."
- "I've worked in situations where the pastor and I differed on whether or not to address disturbing issues. He preferred to avoid such things out of fear of people's reaction. I was much more willing to speak up."

When I invited participants to describe an experience of listening to preaching during a crisis, several commented about the preaching they heard following the attacks on September 11, 2001. One vaguely described experiences that disappointed because they were not linked to scripture, but added that other times when hearing preaching in crisis, the preacher offered hope in God's presence. Several referred to the clergy sexual misconduct scandals. Half of the listener group could not recall hearing an effective sermon or homily presented during a crisis. But some ministers responded with strong memories and feelings:

- "When I was a child, a homily I still remember was delivered by our assistant pastor on a local 'Open Housing' issue. It must have been quite effective for me to still remember it over thirty-five years later."
- "I heard a homily preached by a Catholic priest (my pastor) on the issue of the scandal in the priesthood and the abuse of children by priests. He named the horror in proper terms and condemned it in very strong terms. He explained how, as a priest,

he personally felt and how the Church is wounded and suffering because of the evil of the actions and the evil perpetrated by the U.S. bishops. He squarely placed himself in the pews next to the mothers and fathers who were angry that they had been betrayed by their priests and by the institution of the Church. It was very effective and very well received."

- "Especially the 9/11 crisis when most sermons I heard were opportunistic and emotional and could not be classified as preaching. Most of the preachers were unprepared and showed little or no professionalism."

I asked participants to share their thoughts on the relationship between preaching when the news disturbs and pastoral care. A few respondents seemed to have difficulty relating to the concept of offering pastoral care during the course of their preaching. However, the listener group uniformly affirmed the need for pastoral preaching, although a few cautioned against taking sides. Some advocated finding balance in making the Gospel relevant in today's world. Among the notable comments were these:

- "We need training in this."
- "The people need calm, rational, and religion-based interpretation of events."
- "Preaching is guidance. In crisis we turn to our leaders for guidance. Especially our pastors."
- "I would never be able to meet individually with all the people who come to worship on Sunday. As such, addressing disturbing news topics becomes a powerful means of providing pastoral care in a general way."

I would go even further by stating that preaching is an essential part of the pastoral care of the congregation. As ministers and preachers we cannot avoid the news since we live in the same world as our assemblies and congregations. We have to be impacted as they are and minister to them in their hurt, anger, and fear. When we stand in the pulpit, we stand as one of them, wrestling and struggling to make sense out of the news, helping them to see God in the midst of all. If we don't, we risk splitting what we do in church from the rest of our lives.

When I asked for suggestions for preachers who need to prepare to preach when the community is disturbed by the news or is in the midst of a local crisis, the respondents offered profound ideas. They urged preachers to be sensitive and attentive to the community, to prepare for preaching by reflecting and praying with the congregation, to stay connected to scripture, to be honest with their feelings, to console and avoid judging, to remember God's love and grace, and to be priestly and prophetic. The listener group advised preachers to provide stability, to respect all views, to become informed through several news sources, to emphasize healing in the congregation, and to pray for wisdom.

I wondered whether participants shared my view that preachers should be well informed on a wide range of subjects, so I asked them to check off specific topics that I listed. Several checked off all the areas: local issues, national issues, international issues, liberation theologies (struggles against injustice in the light of faith), economic trends, politics, popular culture, ecology and environmental issues, basic psychology theory, family dynamics, and world religions. While politics, economic trends, world religions, and popular culture were left off a few questionnaires, one individual checked off liberation theology as the only required knowledge area. Ecology and environmental issues and liberation theologies were checked least often. Write-in areas included Islam, justice and peace issues, church teaching, science, medicine, and the arts, especially theater, science, ethics, and theology.

The last question asked whether a preacher should be a "mediator of the news and the Good News." Responders said they needed to be challenged to apply the "Good News" in our "nitty-gritty" lives and also become informed about the hard realities that call for organized Christian action. Several suggested that preachers approach becoming a mediator of the news and the Good News by carefully balancing the news with scripture and church teachings.

The forty-five people who responded to the questionnaire affirmed my belief that preachers should deal with the news that disturbs from the pulpit. They felt that people need pastoral care during unsettled times and that preachers can offer this in conjunction with the scriptural and sacramental traditions. Do you agree? For your reflection, the questionnaire is found in appendix D.

2

The News as Commerce

Business people need to understand that ownership of a news company involves special, civic responsibilities. Consolidation and cost-cutting may be good for the bottom line in the short term, but it isn't necessarily good for the country or the health of the news business in the long-term... To my mind, what best would serve the country and the free press, is to encourage ownership by entities that are dedicated to public service: *—Companies that invest for the long haul and will serve their communities rather than just ever-greater profits.*[1]

WALTER CRONKITE

Buyouts of major newspapers over the past few years by wealthy investors within and outside the media industry have changed journalistic expectations, as well as operations. When the Chicago-based Tribune Company bought the *Los Angeles Times,* it planned to dismantle its acquisition's reporting operations overseas and downsize the newspaper from a leading national paper to a regional news provider. The paper's staff and readers overwhelmingly rejected that proposal, for they took pride in their paper's quality and knew that having too few reporters in the field could endanger diversity of thought and perspective.[2] For them, serving the community meant upholding an excellent standard of journalism. Tribune Company's current CEO, Sam Zell, who acquired the Tribune Co., the parent company of the *Times* in December 2007, considers his holdings, which include eleven newspapers and twenty-three television stations in several major cities, as investments, criticizing journalists for reporting on news the public doesn't want to read.[3] He has cut more than 400 positions since taking the helm.

Such stories and other information in this chapter may cause you to question the validity and reliability of the news accounts you receive. Becoming media literate requires that we understand media's business interests as well as the public service media provide. A media corporation's focus on the bottom line may lead to cost-cutting measures that result in superficial news coverage or news-gathering that relies on increasingly limited sources. For example, it's costly to put reporters on the ground, and many newspapers have followed the Tribune in merging resources and cutting the number of staff reporters in the field, instead subscribing to wire service reports, reprinting press releases and reprinting news stories from larger city papers.[4]

While in-depth reporting and analysis in our newspapers would help us better understand complex stories, more publishers are copying the *USA Today* and television and radio news broadcasting format that essentially delivers sound bites in print. Tim McGuire, former editor and senior vice president of the *Star Tribune* in Minneapolis, now a faculty member at Arizona State University's Walter Cronkite School of Journalism and Mass Communications, raised concerns that not only do these shortcuts provide less coverage and ultimately a news product with less quality, but also that using unmodified, unattributed press releases has become a persistent ethical issue over the past fifteen years.[5]

When news coverage is skimpy, preachers, like everyone else, need to put considerable effort into understanding important issues. For me, that means reading my local newspaper, plus at least one national paper online, watching local and national newscasts, and listening to National Public Radio during my commuting time. It's clear that to become well informed, I need to gather information from news outlets with different perspectives.

Business, Entertainment, and News

I grew to adulthood during the era of the *CBS Nightly News* with Walter Cronkite. During the two decades that he was managing editor and anchor, Cronkite was America's icon of integrity. After he retired from newscasting in 1981, before personal computers and the Internet, cable television, and cell phones transformed communication, Cronkite remained an active observer and commentator, frequently asked to speak about media and the free press.

In the decades following his tenure as America's preeminent broadcaster, the media industry has become much more complicated and competitive. Large media corporations continue to expand through mergers and consolidations. Their portfolios include television, radio, newspapers, magazines, film, music, and retail product lines often related to their entertainment offerings. News departments, previously subsidized by networks in the public interest, are expected to turn a profit. Mass media's bottom line is driven by a variety of other factors, including the corporate philosophy of the executives and board of directors, advertising sponsorships, public taste, and politics.

Local television newscasts provide an excellent service, but like local papers they pay scant attention to world events. However, even the major networks and 24-hour cable news providers cater to a public more fascinated by coverage of celebrities than by insightful news reporting of national and international events. Sometimes what passes for news is merely interesting or sensational trivia, no doubt due to the 24-hour news cycle that has the luxury of rehashing relatively unimportant items. There were many examples of this during the 2008 Democratic Party primaries, when candidate gaffes occupied the airways to the detriment of substantive policy discussions. To the credit of citizens and the media industry, there was considerable criticism when ABC hosts spent the first 50 minutes of a major debate between the two leading contenders dealing with the issues of Sen. Obama's wearing or not wearing a flag pin and Sen. Clinton's exaggeration of her arrival in Bosnia.[6]

When we want to receive accurate and complete information about critical stories, not only do we need to consult a broad array of news sources produced by print, broadcast, and Internet media, but we also need to become aware of the marketing niches and agendas of these media outlets. Financially motivated corporate executives determine the particular formats, content, and delivery styles for reporting the news. Stories are "spun" to appeal to particular audiences, and the information may be slanted toward the political and economic views of the media corporation's owner or board of directors. As media corporations have gained power and influence, thoughtful citizens question the quality of news reporting, expressing concern over what is omitted, as well as what is produced.

News and Politics

The First Amendment to the U.S. Constitution guarantees the right to a free press. However, at times in our nation's history, administrations have manipulated or withheld information because of national security concerns or political agendas. Aided by additional distance from the early part of the twenty-first century, historians will be better able to analyze and interpret the data about how information was communicated and spun during the period prior to the Iraq War. Some media professionals have claimed that the White House stifled dissenting news stories by calling them unpatriotic. For example, in the documentary *Buying the War*, former Chairman and CEO of CNN Walter Isaacson revealed how he prevented the airing of material that ran counter to the Bush administration's policy:[7]

Walter Isaacson: There was a patriotic fervor and the administration used it so that if you challenged anything you were made to feel that there was something wrong with that. And there was even almost a patriotism police which, you know, they'd be up there on the Internet sort of picking anything a Christiane Amanpour, or somebody else would say as if it were disloyal...

Bill Moyers: We interviewed a former reporter at CNN who had been there through that period. And this reporter said this quote, "Everybody on staff just sort of knew not to push too hard to do stories critical of the Bush Administration."

Walter Isaacson: Especially right after 9/11. Especially when the war in Afghanistan is going on. There was a real sense that you don't get that critical of a government that's leading us in wartime.

Bill Moyers: When American forces went after the terrorist bases in Afghanistan, network and cable news reported the civilian casualties...the patriot police came knocking.

Walter Isaacson: We'd put it on the air and by nature of a twenty-four–hour TV network, it was replaying over and over again. So, you would get phone calls. You would get advertisers. You would get the Administration.

Bill Moyers: You said pressure from advertisers?

Walter Isaacson: Not direct pressure from advertisers, but big people in corporations were calling up and saying, "You're being anti-American here."

Bill Moyers: So Isaacson sent his staff a memo, leaked to *The Washington Post*: "It seems perverse" he said, "to focus too much on the casualties or hardship in Afghanistan." And he ordered his reporters and anchors to balance the images of civilian devastation with reminders of September 11th.

Walter Isaacson: I felt if we put into context, we could alleviate the pressure of people saying, "Don't even show what's happening in Afghanistan."

Reporters from Knight Ridder appearing in that same program told how their stories critical of the administration's intelligence on Iraq were either not run in the papers that subscribed to their service or they were buried in the back pages.

Consider how preachers might have been more influential if they had received all the information available to the Knight Ridder reporters. Informed preachers, their congregations and their elected members of Congress who also lacked complete and accurate information, might have been able to press for a delay in military action.

Ethical Issues and the Free Press

When family members offered different versions of a story, my beloved Aunt Mimi often paraphrased that old Chinese proverb: There's your truth, my truth, and the real truth. Like the stories we tell about our personal lives, what we hear or watch in media is told from the producer's perspective. For example, political bias has been around as long as we have had communication media. When newspapers were the only major players, the publishers' political leanings were well known; and editorials often supported candidates or policies. The public knew where the papers stood on issues. In our competitive mass media era, when media try to appeal to as wide an audience as possible, news stories may be framed more subtly to align with a particular editorial position or corporate bias without the consumers' knowledge.

With the development and influence of mass media and the growth and power of the megacorporations that own them, ethical issues have emerged as the move toward business-centered media versus public-interest-centered media has revolutionized the industry.

In 1987, in an effort to set standards and prevent unethical broadcast news practices, the Radio-Television News Directors Association adopted the seven standards of the "RTNDA Code of Broadcast News Ethics." The opening statement reads: "The responsibility of radio and television journalists is to gather and report information of importance and interest to the public accurately, honestly and impartially."[8] The main problem with this mission statement is that an individual or select group of people within a media outlet chooses what is important and of interest to the public. The first standard states: "Strive to present the source or nature of broadcast news material in a way that is balanced, accurate and fair." A statement directed toward those who prepare news for presentation says: "They will evaluate information solely on its merits as news, rejecting sensationalism or misleading emphasis in any form."

A sense of urgency or crisis drives ratings. To catch the attention of the public, which can result in increased advertising revenue and more favorable positioning in the media marketplace, network and cable television producers may choose to air violent or controversial stories and present issues dramatically. The axiom, "If it bleeds, it leads," rules in promo spots that lead up to television newscasts. Have you noticed how the graphics and sound accompanying these promos heighten the drama and persuade you to stay tuned?

Many of the ethical issues and concerns about today's media were discussed by broadcast professionals decades ago. As communications theorist Lee Thayer and colleagues noted in a 1980 collection of essays, Americans are accustomed to hearing the news presented dramatically in black-and-white terms, so news producers provide sound bites that make the stories seem less complex than they are. Former ABC broadcaster Sander Vanocur decried the institutionalization of simplistic news programming, claiming that those who write at this level perceive their viewers as unable to handle material of some complexity.[9] It takes a great deal of skill to present complex material so that most people can understand it, as well as to make it interesting enough to hold their attention. Writing in 1971, when President Nixon was president, Vanocur had the same concerns that we raise now about the integrity and completeness of the news we receive. He claimed that networks were trying to avoid problems with the government over their reporting of sensitive stories. Decades later this same issue continues to threaten the flow of information.[10]

Pulitzer Prize winner Harry S. Ashmore, known for his contributions toward ending segregation, once described all journalistic institutions as "organs of the Establishment."[11] He claimed that "In a capitalistic society they enjoy guarantees against state control and are expected to perform a critical role, but their economic dependence upon the prevailing system establishes fixed limits to the range of dissent… they cannot be revolutionary…."[12]

The late conservative commentator Leslie Stone, of the BBC's *World Service,* was convinced that the news is not supposed to be neutral. He believed his mission as a journalist was to inform, persuade, and entertain, both to hold the attention of the audience and communicate to people in different societies.[13] Blogger Cenk Uygur of the *The Huffington Post* agrees with a twist:

> The media isn't supposed to be neutral–it is supposed to be objective. There is an enormous difference between the two. And this is a difference that has been lost on the mainstream media for quite awhile now… Truth exists. It is supposed to

be the job of the press to try to find it and report it to the best
of their abilities. It is not their job to try to create an artificial
neutral reality. [14]

The news we receive is not neutral because even when the facts
are presented objectively, we will form our own opinions based on
our individual experiences and biases. Media literate consumers will
understand their own biases and observe biases in reporting that
appear to persuade consumers to respond positively or negatively.
Consider that much of the world gets its news about the United States
from CNN International. Are the people of Middle Eastern Islamic
countries receiving an accurate picture of American people through
the lens of CNN? Are *you* represented by its images and stories? Do
media create and/or shape our identity and the identities of others? On
the other hand, when we watch programming about another culture,
do we draw conclusions about that culture from the reporting?

In the United States, we seldom encounter the work of journalists
who report from news bureaus of other countries, especially those
who may at times be critical of U.S. policies. Isolated from the world
press, except for the BBC where it's available, not only are we likely
to be under-informed about world situations, but we can easily remain
naïve about the world's perception of America. For insights about
our image abroad, we can take advantage of www.Watchingamerica.
com, a nonpartisan Web site offering world opinion through articles
translated from the foreign newspapers, providing a link to English
newspapers from countries around the world. [15]

Perhaps overreacting and fearful that Al-Jazeera's English channel service, which debuted in 2006, would be a "mouthpiece for
terrorists, including al Qaida's Osama bin Laden," lobbyists in the
U.S. influenced cable and satellite station owners against carrying
it. [16] While several cable managers cited a lack of demand for
"foreign-centric news" in the U.S., a few small cable operators in
Houston, Ohio, Vermont, and Washington D.C. offer the channel.
Seen in 100 million households worldwide after one year of service,
the channel has a big following in Israel, despite the separately run
Arabic language Al-Jazeera channel's frequent negative criticism of
Israel and the West. Upon hiring prominent journalists from Western
countries, often away from major media outlets, the new broadcasting
service staffed newsrooms in Doha, Kuala Lumpur, London, and
Washington, with twenty bureaus worldwide. Instead of reducing
their field reporting as a number of other media outlets have done,
they've increased it, competing with the BBC for the numbers of
reporters on the ground.

When the *International Herald Tribune*'s Roger Cohen discussed the channel in an Op-Ed piece in *The New York Times*, he made a strong case for media literacy concluding that "(c)omparative courses in how Al Jazeera, CNN, the BBC, and U.S. networks portray the Iraq war and the Israeli-Palestinian conflict should be taught in all U.S. high schools and colleges. Al Jazeera English should be widely and readily available."[17] More than 400 people posted comments on his blog, such as these:

…We must be willing to face and understand philosophies and behaviors that are different from ours. Providing our children the "critical thinking" skills this new century requires is essential for the future well being of this nation. Hence, a mandatory comparative media course at all levels of the educational system is a wonderful and interesting way to ensure that our children possess both the critical thinking skills and realistic perspective on themselves, their country, and other nations.[18]

Terrorists or no terrorists, information about other peoples, cultures, and points of view is invaluable in transforming "the Other" into a reasonable, or at least understandable, fellow human.[19]

David Marash, formerly with ABC and one of the most high-profile journalists to join the staff of Al Jazeera English in February 2006, resigned his position in March 2008 when he was reassigned from the anchor desk to a special correspondent role. In an extended interview with the *Columbia Journalism Review*, Marash described his reasons for leaving, citing in particular his perception of an increasing anti-American bias:

It got to the point where I feel that in a globe where Al Jazeera sets a very, very high reporting standard, and a very, very high standard for both numerical and qualitative and authentic staffing, that the United States was becoming a serious exception to their role, and a place where the journalism did not measure up to the standards that were set almost everywhere else by Al Jazeera English's very fine reporting. …And the coverage of Latin America and Africa in particular is just so terrific… you would want to watch it for that alone. But you know, the thing that I loved best about the original concept, was the sort of fugue of points of view and opinions, because I think that's what desperately needed in the world. We need to know, for example, in America, how angry the rest of the world is at Americans. Our own news media tend to shelter us from this very unpleasant news.[20]

With the hire of Tony Burman, a former editor-in-chief of the Canadian Broadcasting Company, who has begun serving as managing director, arriving shortly after Marash's departure, perhaps the issues of objectivity and American editorial input will be addressed.[21]

With so much potential that important points about the news may be suppressed, incomplete, inaccurate, or biased in different ways, more than being well-informed as responsible citizens, preachers intending to promote Jesus' Gospel of peace and justice throughout the world must especially seek out diverse sources from which to glean and corroborate the truth.

Globalization of Mass Media

Ben Bagdikian, an expert on the process of media mergers and consolidation leading to the globalization of media, documented the development of mass media corporations and the implications of their increasing influence:

> In the 1980s a handful of giant private organizations began to dominate the world's mass media. Their goal was to control by the end of the century most of the world's important newspapers, magazines, books, broadcast stations, movies, recordings, and video-cassettes. The possibilities of misusing such control of what are sometimes called the "cultural industries" should make all thoughtful people pause: the lords of the global village have their own political agenda. All resist economic changes that do not support their financial interests. Together, they exert a homogenizing power over ideas, culture and commerce that affects populations larger than any in history. Neither Caesar nor Hitler, Franklin Roosevelt nor any Pope, has commanded as much power to shape the information on which so many people depend to make decisions about everything from whom to vote for to what to eat.[22]

Each update of Bagdikian's *The Media Monopoly* revealed further consolidation of the corporations controlling media. In 1983, he gave a figure of fifty. By 1987, he said there were twenty-six; in 1990, twenty-three; in 1996, ten; and just five when he released *The New Media Monopoly*, in 2004.[23] Those five conglomerates are: Time Warner (the largest media firm in the world); The Walt Disney Company; Murdoch's News Corporation (based in Australia); Viacom; and Bertelsmann (based in Germany).[24] The holdings of each of the five top megacorporations include print and electronic media, film and book publishing.[25]

A tremor went through the news media industry in 2007 when Rupert Murdoch purchased Dow Jones & Company for $5 billion from the Bancroft family, adding *The Wall Street Journal* to his business news properties. Some questioned whether his conservative political views would influence the editorial content of that venerable paper. Murdoch's news industry holdings in the United States also include *The New York Post*, Fox Television Network, and the Internet site MySpace. Murdoch agreed to refrain from interfering with the paper's editorial independence, though his purchase permitted him to introduce business changes.[26] Writing years earlier in *The Atlantic*, James Fallows predicted how he thought Murdoch would influence the future of news media:

> Two principles that others can take from Murdoch's experience are his total market-mindedness and his pragmatic embrace of politics...Sooner or later Murdoch's outlets, especially Fox News, will be more straightforward about their political identity—and they are likely to bring the rest of the press with them...Our journalistic culture may soon enough resemble that of early nineteenth-century America, in which party-owned newspapers presented selective versions of the truth. News addressed to a particular niche—not simply in its content but also in its politics—may be the natural match to an era with hundreds of satellite and cable channels and limitless numbers of Internet sites...One way or another, self-governing societies must figure out the suitable commercial channels through which the information necessary for democratic decisions can be spread.[27]

As for holding in tension the responsibility of the press to serve the public interest and that of the corporation to conduct a profitable business, Fallows predicted that the business interests would win out.[28] If the public interest has now become subservient to business in terms of newsgathering and production, the public must learn how to respond appropriately to protect the freedom of the press.

Government Regulation of Mass Media

Since the 1980s, the government has loosened its regulations on mass media. In 1985, the Federal Communications Commission permitted media corporations to own up to twelve stations, an increase from the seven previously allowed. In 1987, the FCC eliminated the Fairness Doctrine, which meant that stations no longer needed to present opposing viewpoints on critical issues. Moving toward globalization of media, the 1996 Telecommunications Act permitted the creation of huge media corporations that could legally hold interests in all forms of media. By 1999, the FCC paved the way for corporations to own more than one station in sizable United States cities. Many have lamented that this process gives media corporations even more control over the distribution of information and a variety of products.

Let's examine the contents of Disney's portfolio. In January 2000, it owned ABC, ten local television stations, forty-four radio stations, *Discover Magazine*, Miramax Films, and Hyperion Books.[29] By 2007 Disney continued to own ABC and ten local television stations. It increased its holdings that now included nineteen more radio stations, four music production companies, four book imprinting companies with several subdivisions, fifteen magazines, five Disney resorts and parks, Walt Disney Pictures, Touchstone Pictures, Hollywood Pictures, Miramax Films, Buena Vista Home Entertainment, and Pixar. In addition, Disney owns Buena Vista Theatrical Productions, The Disney Store, Disney Cruise Line, ESPN Zone, Disney Toys, The Baby Einstein Company, and Walt Disney Internet Group.[30]

Most of the deregulation has occurred quietly at the Federal Communications Commission, with little public input. Commissioner Michael Copps was quoted as saying during his tenure on the FCC:

> If you take this to its logical conclusion, you could end up with a situation where one company owns the newspaper, the television station, the radio station, and the cable system... That may have some economic efficiencies attached to it, but I daresay it also has some profound democratic and social and political considerations that we ignore only at our own tremendous peril.[31]

Pollsters discovered that 72 percent of the people they surveyed knew nothing about the FCC plans and only 4 percent knew a great deal about them.[32] Brian Lambert, a media columnist in the Twin Cities, was sharply critical about the lack of reporting done by the national media on the deregulation issue:

> Fundamentally, the problem with telling the FCC story is that the average person has a hard time relating to it. It is abstract and bureaucratic. There are no pictures.... No corpse. No sex...The paucity of coverage of this issue, something that

will directly affect every American virtually every minute of their lives, illuminates what may be critics' primary concern, namely lack of diversity of information.[33]

An important change in the rules that the FCC has been debating for several years is to allow a company cross-ownership, that is, to permit a media corporation to hold both television or radio and a newspaper in most markets. How might that influence political issues covered by the local television station? In Indianapolis, the NBC affiliate WTHR and the Gannett newspaper *The Indianapolis Star* share a significant news-reporting relationship. In several cities Gannett already owns both a newspaper and television station. Consumers should at least be aware that media owned by the same corporation will present news from a similar perspective, affecting what stories are produced and how they are told.[34]

Deregulation has increased the need for consumers to be more critical and perhaps skeptical about the news they receive. Corporate buyouts of media outlets can result in cost efficiency to the detriment of the product. When fewer reporters are sent to remote regions, more footage and still photos are purchased from sources in the field, and stock videos are reused. Media consolidation lets the company's bottom line influence the style and integrity of newscasts. Already a tabloid approach to print and broadcast journalism prevails. Why? Surveys show that people want to be entertained and are captivated by human-interest stories with which they can identify. Broadcast personalities are employed to attract "consumers." Perhaps I'm not alone in thinking that I'm simply an object for advertisers. Sad but true, when media focus on financials at the expense of content, much television programming is simply filler, the material between the commercials. Likewise, the news stories in my city paper are fitted around large, colorful, irregularly-shaped advertisements. These ads attract the eye before the reader encounters the smaller, strangely configured news articles.

With consolidation the local community could lose its distinctive voice. It will become increasingly more difficult for local or independent producers to be heard as media giants stake out their territories. While the FCC was preparing to vote in late 2007 to permit more deregulation, which would permit media ownership of newspapers and broadcasting in the same market, lobbyists working against further deregulation attracted supporters in both the House and Senate to investigate the impact of cross-ownership on local news, public affairs, and cultural programming within a given market and provide for more citizen input.[35] The commissioners' vote prepared the way for cross-ownership of newspapers and broadcast outlets in the top twenty markets as long as eight independent media outlets remained in the particular market and the broadcast units available for purchase were not among the top four performers of these independent outlets. In addition, the FCC also considered in the public interest cross-ownership in the smaller markets if seven hours of local news was added or if the particular media outlet for sale had fiscal problems.[36]

While the FCC ruled in favor of big media, a citizens' campaign against the decision snowballed into a "media reform movement." Senators joined in a bipartisan effort to support hundreds of thousands of Americans who protested the enactment of the FCC ruling. The senators moved to nullify the FCC's media consolidation process in May, 2008, although at this writing, the congressional "pushback" will require a vote in the House.[37]

Another large issue requiring legislation that has considerable ramifications for our future access to information on the Internet is "net neutrality." The "Internet Freedom and Nondiscrimination Act of 2008" was introduced in Congress on May 8, 2008 "to promote competition, to facilitate trade, and to ensure competitive and nondiscriminatory access to the Internet."[38] Net neutrality assumes that all providers will permit all information to travel unimpeded on the Internet at the same speed without being held up or slowed down. Corporate providers want to charge customers for priority services or restrict customers to their own products. For those of us who spend much of our professional and personal time communicating with others or benefiting from the vast information contained on the World Wide Web, we will need to follow the legislative process and make our voices heard.[39]

Television News from the McCarthy Hearings to *60 Minutes* to the Fox News Channel

Simply by airing the Army-McCarthy hearings in 1954, television molded public discourse.[40] McCarthy began to lose credibility as the hearings went on day after day. When President Kennedy was assassinated in 1963, continuous television reporting held the country together as a new president was sworn in. Coverage of the Kennedy tragedy became the focal point for the citizens of the country to grieve together. During the 1960s television became the most popular medium for news, when major stories of the civil rights movement and the Vietnam War received a great deal of coverage. A significant outcome of the extensive battlefield reporting from Vietnam was the government's prohibition of television cameras during subsequent military actions.[41]

In stark contrast to the government's censorship of battlefield photography following the Vietnam War, from the outset of the war in Iraq in 2003 the public received real-time images from the field. The freedom of "embedded" journalists to report from the battlefield, albeit within certain predetermined parameters, has itself generated considerable discussion about media ethics.

Photojournalism produces powerful images capable of molding opinion, which can motivate citizens to challenge government policy. There may be no greater example of this than the photograph in the May 1972 edition of *Life Magazine* picturing the naked girl, Phan Thi Kim Phuc, who was shot as she was running from napalm. Years later a former special counsel to President Richard Nixon, Charles Colson, reflected on this image:

> The image earned the photographer a Pulitzer Prize and helped turn the heart of a nation against the war. But for me there was no escaping a sense of personal responsibility. The photo was scorched permanently into my memory, whispering the haunting question. Was I responsible for policies that led to this small child's agony?[42]

Is Colson's question vital to us today? I believe that preachers of the Gospel of Jesus must take responsibility for obtaining reliable information about the news and respond by taking a stand, either affirming or criticizing as the situation requires.

During the Vietnam era, CBS producer Don Hewitt created the innovative *60 Minutes*. A "hybrid" news program, *60 Minutes* developed longer, in-depth segments based on current events and personalities in the news than could be presented on nightly broadcasts. As the magazine format became profitable, it was duplicated by the other networks which also discovered that news divisions could meet financial goals without needing to be subsidized.[43] Hewitt affirmed this in a late 1990s interview:

> *60 Minutes* destroyed television by equating news with the profit motive; news organizations sought money in magazine and entertainment news programs, reducing their long-standing, and expensive, commitments to breaking news. But Hewitt set the groundwork. His blunt statements suggesting that success depends on marketing, and his continuous refinements of the product often generated controversy.

Audiences must experience stories in the pit of their stomach, the narrative must take the viewer by the throat, and, noted Hewitt, when a segment is over it's not significant what they have been told–'only what they remember of what you tell them.'[44]

Previously, news divisions were expected to compete on the basis of the integrity of the content of their journalism. Unfortunately, when news programming began to make money, profitability began to drive both local and network news. In the 1970s the ratings "sweeps" periods drove competing networks to gain audience share, which resulted in more revenue from sponsors. From that point on, news programs have become self-conscious reminders of how the public responds to the personalities of newscasters and the violent or sensational stories that lead typical broadcasts rather than in-depth information. Fox Cable News is a good example of creating niche market-share based on its personalities who have developed a combatant style of conversation that is often just marginally civil but has proven to be extremely popular. Contrast Fox's niche with that of "The News Hour with Jim Lehrer" on PBS, which provides news headlines followed by in-depth interviews featuring experts who comment and provide background on current critical issues. However, the venerable public television news program, despite its audience of 1.2 million adults nightly, is struggling financially. With certain longtime sponsorships ending and a decline in corporate advertising generally, PBS has been developing funding sources that prefer to underwrite shorter projects or programming for a limited time period. In addition, corporate sponsors are choosing to support specific pieces of the News Hour's programming, such as overseas reports.[45]

A Discussion about Corporate Influence on Local Newspapers

To understand more about corporate and political influence as it affects local print media, I interviewed Dan Carpenter, editorial staff writer and columnist with *The Indianapolis Star*, which is owned by Gannett Company, Inc., and James Patterson, a former editorial staff writer and columnist with that paper. I learned a great deal from these working journalists who were eager to tell their story.[46]

When I asked about any constraints on their reporting, both agreed that time and space, based on business and demographics, were considerations, with perceived reader interest driving content. They called my attention to the amount of print and graphics devoted to the Colts, Indianapolis' football team, indicating that sports is really the paper's bread and butter. While some of the sports teams' games even make the front page, which was uncommon years ago, much news from overseas is relegated to inside pages as briefs.

As for national stories, editors choose from the reporting of corporate Gannett writers, Associated Press or from major newspapers throughout the country. However, covering local events requires that an editor be familiar with the issues, including guest speakers who come to town. Dan remembered that when Coretta Scott King came to speak, the middle level editor explicitly decided not to cover her because she hadn't been in the news lately, and he didn't think the readers cared. For Dan, an event with Coretta Scott King should have been covered automatically, at least for a small story.

The reporters have noticed that their working relationships are much more "top-down" than they used to be. Formerly, reporters and editors exchanged ideas, and a reporter could tell the editor he or she was going to cover a particular story. Today, editors come up with the ideas and assign the stories.

I asked how television influences the newspaper business, James said that *The Indianapolis Star* favored *USA Today*'s philosophy to print shorter stories, with more visuals, graphics, and pictures. Dan said they were frantically trying to market to the 18–24 and 24–35 age groups. He believes that a newspaper is always trying to get people's attention, not necessarily challenging them with new ways of looking at the world, adding that this (short-sighted) way of thinking may have implications for preaching as well. We'll explore more of their thoughts along these lines in chapter 6.

The News Business and Propaganda

Quentin J. Schultze, a communications professor and author, who critiques media from a Christian perspective, believes that human communication is a gift from God.[47] He's concerned that the globalization of media leads local communities to lose a sense of *orality* within their distinctive culture.[48] By this he means that the interpersonal relationships of speaking and listening are threatened by media because media tend to transmit all the ideas people are intended to have.

Schultze coined the term *priestly media*, suggesting that media "powerfully confirm and exploit what a tribe wants to believe."[49] Taking the Latin word *pontifex*, and translating it as *bridge-builder*, Schultze holds that ideally "media build bridges that connect us to one another and to the broader beliefs of our culture."[50] We have seen this in our country's darkest moments, when media have become very patriotic during wartime or sympathetic to victims during natural disasters. But Schultze also noticed that mass media tend to focus on the general homogenous community and leave out specific cultural groups or traditions. An example of such an omission was the contributions of Hispanic-Americans in the extensive Second World War documentary produced by Ken Burns in 2007. When Latino columnist Ruben Navarrette chided the noted filmmaker for failing to include the participation of Hispanic-Americans, Burns was persuaded to add interviews with Hispanic veterans to his multi-part series.[51]

If mass media is failing to include everyone in our society, this can become even more problematic in the future as fewer minorities are operating local television stations and will continue to be less visible in the industry if local stations continue to be absorbed by large media corporations.

Jacques Ellul's book *Propagandes* influenced Schultze's philosophy of mass media. A "renaissance man" with many academic interests, including theology, politics, and sociology, Ellul defined propaganda as a system that conditions people to believe in certain ways. With its partial truths, propaganda brings current trends into sharp focus. Propaganda may consist of subtle manipulations of the truth, such as half-truths, limited truths and out-of-context truths.[52] Schultze suggests that priestly media, that is, mass media, propagandize because they seek conformity. Both Schultze and Ellul, the latter never a friend of new technologies, came to believe that the media's only interest is in molding the audience for commercial purposes and that the development of mass media provided the means for using the techniques of propaganda in the broader society.[53]

Although many media critics and journalists agree that commerce drives the industry, most journalists remain detached from those business interests and are intensely dedicated to providing the best quality news gathering, production, and presentation to the public, despite the realities of the business environment. Certainly the perception that for-profit media manipulate their audiences might move us to make teaching the principles of media literacy mandatory in the school and highly recommended for adults as well. Parents, teachers, preachers, and others who take responsibility for shaping ethics and morals are on the frontline of this process to form *media-literate* consumers.

What Does the Future Hold for the News Business?

While financial woes continue to plague newspapers, managements are investing heavily in their online potential, with Web sites that provide much of the paper's print content, daily e-mails distributed with headlines and major news updates, videos (vlogs[54]) and blogs, plus opportunities for readers to participate in comment or talk back forums. Electronic media staff occupy space alongside reporters and editors in newsrooms. Even television stations refer consumers to their Web sites for additional information on stories. With computers available to so many workers, news is a commodity that is available all the time. There's no need to wait for a newscast or a newspaper. As the Carnegie Corporation's online publication, *The Carnegie Reporter,* concludes:

> ...no future generation of new consumers will fit earlier profiles since their expectations and their habits have changed forever–and technology is a big part of the reason why. "Young people are more curious than ever but define news on their own terms," says Jeff Jarvis, who is president of Advance. net, a unit of Advance Publications, and who publishes a widely read blog, Buzzmachine.com. "They get news where they want it, when they want it. Media is about control now. We used to wait for the news to come to us. Now news waits for us to come to it. That's their expectation. We get news on cable and on the Internet any time, any place."[55]

Banking on the popularity of wireless mobile devices, including smart phones, the Associate Press debuted a news program called *Mobile News Network,* which provides multi-media news from all over the world, sports and entertainment, including videos and photos.[56] Another start-up to watch is *ProPublica,* a not-for-profit, independent, non-partisan newsroom located in Manhattan that will concentrate on investigative journalism, an area currently at risk in some major news organizations. Led by Paul Steiger, former managing editor of the *Wall Street Journal,* and funded by several foundations, *ProPublica* offers a strong mission for justice:

> Our work will focus exclusively on truly important stories, stories with "moral force." We will do this by producing journalism that shines a light on exploitation of the weak by the strong and on the failures of those with power to vindicate the trust placed in them... we face a situation in which sources of *opinion* are proliferating, but sources of *facts* on which those opinions are based are shrinking. The former phenomenon is almost certainly, on balance, a societal good; the latter is surely a problem...In all, this seems like a moment in our history–the history of our country and the history of

journalism—when new models are necessary to carry forward some of the great work of journalism in the public interest that is such an integral part of self-government, and thus an important bulwark of our democracy.[57]

This innovative prospect is good news if funding remains viable over time. Strong foundation support offers hope to a slice of the media industry that has experienced increased difficulty balancing the public interest while maintaining profitability. In this technological transition, perhaps more of us will consider participating in citizen journalism through blogs and informal relationships with news organizations, both print and electronic, thus becoming a part of the future of news media.

3

The Media Literacy Toolbox

The campaign wars are playing out on an entirely new front this time around, as the most enduring and damaging charges and countercharges flourish on the Web. The information, spread through streaming video and e-mail chains—and much of it untrue—is the handiwork of both amateurs and organized partisans, and they won't go away.[1]

GWEN IFILL, *THE NEWS HOUR*

We can all critique media effectively once we understand how media presentations are constructed. A media message includes the following elements:

- Creator/author/producer
- Format and techniques of production
- Audience
- Content or message
- Motive or purpose

These elements are incorporated into the Center for Media Literacy's five "core concepts" and five "key questions" found in their *MediaLit Kit*,™ which was created to help consumers understand and analyze media messages.[2] The Center for Media Literacy has given me permission to use the concepts and questions. I will show how they relate to news media and apply to preaching. The material serves as an organizational skeleton for the chapter, and I will insert additional tools and devices used to construct media messages.

Media literacy began as a grassroots movement. Over forty years ago, parents, educators, and religious leaders began lobbying against violence and explicit sexuality in media, as well as manipulative advertising targeting children and youth. Now all fifty states and the provinces of Canada include media literacy education in school curricula.[3] As well, several colleges and universities offer under-graduate and graduate degrees.

Although we may not be media professionals, we can benefit from understanding the basics of journalism, including media production and presentation. In a real sense, we are all producing information; that is, we process and transmit information based on what we see and hear. We "produce" our thoughts in conversations with others, often composing our own or forwarding e-mails that catch our attention. Some of the messages we receive through typical media inspire us to make decisions, particularly those that deal with products, or social and political issues. Understanding the nuances and subtexts of so many messages from multiple sources requires some discernment on our part. Just as not all art works are good or pleasing, not all media are accurate, tasteful, or well presented.

Who Decides What We See and Hear?

CORE CONCEPT #1: All media messages are *constructed*.

KEY QUESTION #1: Who created this message?

News doesn't simply happen and get reported. Several people within a media outlet consider each story and make decisions, not only whether the story will be included, but also how it will be treated, positioned, what graphics will be used, what background material might introduce it, and who will write the story or represent it on-air. The ingredients used to create the complete story may include interviews, a headline, photos or videos, sound from the story's source, and the music that will introduce the segment. In most cases there is much more material—photographs, video, and lengthier interviews—than can be used in the finished message.

For example, one Good Friday, a reporter and a photographer from *The Indianapolis Star* trailed our small group composed mainly of pastors, activists, and seminarians for two hours as we walked a Stations of the Cross. We lugged a large wooden cross and several large plastic tubs that we used for drums as we stopped several times for prayer and reflection in downtown Indianapolis. The reporter wrote about our "stations," which included rescue missions and war monuments. Some of our comments were quoted in the story. The photographer took many pictures, but the photo that accompanied the story was of a large group of colorfully dressed Knights of Columbus members who led a very traditional Stations of the Cross for several hundred participants in a downtown park. The editor, who supervised the entire Good Friday story, chose a visual of the established institution at prayer rather than a photo of our unusual group of pilgrims. The traditional "look" was pictured. While our more radical observance was not visually illustrated, it provided another dimension to the story.

As I continue to develop my own media literacy skills, I observe carefully by watching, listening, and reading, as though I'm appreciating a work of art. I ask questions about how the message was composed or constructed. Was the material treated in passing or, if considered seriously, was it well documented? Does the story stem from first-person observation, several corroborated sources, third-party information, a government source, a professionally conducted survey, or a scientific discovery revealed at a press conference? Does it appear that information is missing?

Occasionally, broadcast news media air stories too quickly because they want to be the first with breaking news. When a story is rushed to print or to air, journalists may miss a critical piece of the story by failing to confirm sources and the veracity of the claims being made. The cloning hoaxes of 2002 and late 2005, forgotten by now, provide stellar examples.[4] We'll look at a rushed-to-print example in the next section and discover why it received media attention.

How Do the Media Capture My Attention?

CORE CONCEPT #2: Media messages are constructed using a creative language with its own rules.

KEY QUESTION #2: What creative techniques are used to attract my attention?

Language

The Los Angeles Times published an article on June 13, 2008, reporting on a claim from researchers for the Virginia-based Center for Health, Environment & Justice that vinyl shower curtains for sale nationally at major stores give off toxic chemicals containing "high concentrations of chemicals that are linked to liver damage as well as damage to the central nervous, respiratory and reproductive systems." The report's coauthor, Stephen Lester, said that seven chemicals found in the shower curtains had been identified as hazardous by the

Environmental Protection Agency.[5] The study had been conducted to determine what produced that familiar new shower curtain smell.

On June 30, a *New York Times* piece reported that although this story had been picked up by major television and print media, its premise had been debunked by the Consumer Product Safety Commission, which questioned the methods of testing and the science of the study.[6] This follow-up story demonstrated how using particular language will attract the news services' attention. In this case, it was the word "toxic." David B. Armon, the president of PR Newswire, explained that every word in a press release must be chosen carefully, not only for the item to be picked up by media, but also by search engines. When the reporter questioned how this type of story would receive the amount of "bounce" from major news outlets, her consultants revealed that strategic use of language is key. Words like "first, most, fastest, tallest, money, fat, cancer, or sex" are among those most likely to elicit media response.[7]

The "text" of a media message, however, means much more than what is printed or spoken. In fact, the text is the entire message with all its content–words, sound, visuals, and the specific ways in which these are created and employed. Messages can contain multiple "subtexts" designed to appeal psychologically to the several different ways we learn and receive information. Each medium develops its own creative language and communicates news and other messages using different templates and stylistic variations. We can be drawn into the message and become persuaded by it in several ways, as the Center for Media Literacy points out:

> Understanding the grammar, syntax and metaphor system of media language, especially the language of sounds and visuals which can reach beyond the rational to our deepest emotional core, increases our appreciation and enjoyment of media experiences as well as helps us to be less susceptible to manipulation.[8]

Preaching also has its particular language. We should not be surprised that convincing preaching often includes some of the same language structures that media employ. As we observe media messages, particularly news and news commentary, we can learn to use persuasive tools in a positive way, incorporating them into our own "preaching language."

Bob McCannon of the New Mexico Media Literacy Project identified some tools of persuasion used in media presentations.[9] They include symbols, exaggeration and fear, humor, integrity, repetition and negative reinforcement, diversion, herd mentality and bandwagon mode, and timing. The language of persuasion can be incorporated through words, as well as through sound and visuals. When we understand how these techniques are used to persuade within media messages, we can begin to "deconstruct" the messages as part of our growing media literacy. Although some of these techniques are used a great deal more in advertising than in news coverage, most of them are found also in news reporting and political commentary.

Symbols

When Sen. Barack Obama delivered a campaign speech on patriotism in Independence, Missouri, a few days prior to the 2008 Independence Day holiday, he was flanked by large American flags. When political candidates or corporate spokespersons hold press conferences, they use visuals to add to the impact of their message. Sometimes these are backdrops with the logos of the organization. Others may use symbols that may persuade the receiver to accept the message, particularly when their use, which may include scientific evidence, charts and other images, helps to clarify the information.

However, when symbols such as the American flag, the cross, or other symbols of faith or national pride are used as part of news reporting, they can stimulate strong emotional reactions. While the display of flags during Obama's speech was designed to connect Obama with patriotism, the burning of an American flag makes many people angry. Not only do they feel hostile toward the protestors, but they ignore the message. The symbol of the U.S. flag takes on additional meaning for the press. While freedom of the press is guaranteed under the First Amendment, government may prevent press access in certain cases. Photographing flag-draped coffins returning from a war zone is one example. A Department of Defense regulation of 1991 prohibits coverage of the military rituals that are performed just before the dead are transported home.[10]

In a high-profile legal case over a major religious symbol, Alabama's Chief Justice Roy Moore refused to comply with a federal court ruling that required the removal of a 5,280-pound monument of the Ten Commandments from the rotunda of the Alabama Judicial Building to a less public site. Demonstrators protested the court's action, claiming that the Ten Commandments form the basis of law for the United States. Neither Moore nor his supporters were willing to accept the federal court decision that the monument violated the U.S. Constitution's ban on government establishment of religion. As this situation became highly politicized, the symbol of the Ten

Commandments itself became an example of how an icon of faith can become a divisive symbol.[11]

Preachers who comment on the news will notice how using symbols may affect a media message. Certain symbols are especially important to us and to our listeners. Some people call these "hub" symbols. These symbols typically relate to the areas that are closest to our core beliefs, which for many listeners include family, faith, and country.[12]

Exaggeration and Fear

Sen. Hillary Clinton's account of her experience on the tarmac in Bosnia during the 2008 presidential primary campaign was an exaggerated claim, which she made in speeches, as well as in her book.[13] Exaggerated statements distort reality. Sometimes memory or available facts are responsible for misinformation. For example, battlefield accounts or estimated numbers of fatalities from natural disasters are often confusing because reporters may receive conflicting numbers of injuries and deaths. Often unavoidable under the circumstances, these reports may be clarified later. But intentional exaggeration or "hype" leads trusting media consumers to respond negatively to a news story or advertisement based on inflated claims. The public's trust in both government and media was diminished when media reported that the government's claim, based on insufficient intelligence sources, that weapons of mass destruction in Iraq imminently threatened the security of the United States.

Related to exaggeration are stories that play on fear. In my urban community of Indianapolis, when a news story featured Hispanic immigrants, a subsequent account revealed that some people feared these newcomers would take over their jobs. Those interviewed also claimed that these immigrants threatened our security because of their proclivity to engage in criminal activities. A group of American Nazis attempted to intensify this fear when they sponsored a rally at the State Capitol building. Fortunately, the press provided balance by covering the much larger celebration of diversity that countered the Nazis' rally.[14] A highly charged issue, immigration continues to elicit fear and intolerance on local and national levels, as the press continues to transmit the public's concerns that those in the country illegally use educational, health, and social services disproportionately, at taxpayers' expense. With reports of problems associated with immigration more frequent than suggestions for positive solutions to the issue, the level of frustration remains high.

Since 9/11, ethnic scapegoating has frequently made headlines. In a similar way as the country's response to people of Japanese ancestry in World War II, the loyalty of people of Arab descent was questioned. Some were ostracized by fearful people within their towns and cities, some even incarcerated for years without trials under the USA Patriot Act. This encouraged some people to conclude that those accused of subversion who happen to be of Arab or Muslim background are guilty until proven innocent. Only later was the public informed about false arrests and the substandard conditions in which people were being held. Media counteract fear and intolerance when *they* use the tool of persuasion to portray Muslim-Americans as people who share similar values and pursuits as most Americans.

A local issue moved me to become more active in tolerance education in late 2007. Our airport is served by many religiously observant Muslim taxi drivers who perform a ritual washing before daily prayers. When a news release from the airport management noted that special footbaths would be installed in the new airport that's under construction, a minister's protest—which expanded to include his congregation and some other clergy—captured the interest of the media. While couched in constitutional terms, the pastor's rhetoric signaled his intolerance and fear. Although the public was sympathetic to him because he had lost a son who fought in Iraq, the latent fears and prejudice of hundreds of people in the community were exposed as they weighed in online about the project, which was to be funded privately.[15]

Early in 2007, when Sen. Barack Obama was preparing to announce his candidacy for the Democratic nomination for president, he quickly became the target of a smear campaign by irresponsible journalists who claimed that he attended a madrassa in Indonesia as a child. First printed in a magazine owned by the *Washington Times*, the undocumented story circulated widely on the Internet and on the Fox News Channel until CNN exposed it.[16] I recall receiving an unattributed e-mail that grew out of this story and was circulated widely as part of an agenda to discredit Obama. I researched the story and sent a message to both the person who had forwarded the false e-mail and her list of addressees. I pointed out that at the very least, when messages are not attributed to individuals, recipients should not forward them. To investigate such stories and a variety of hoaxes, we can begin by consulting www.snopes.com, a Web site that verifies information and dismisses false claims.

Beyond misstatements and emotionally laden campaigns by individuals, a real issue for the media is the prevalence of exaggerated rhetoric and outright lies as political tools to exploit the public's fear. So many rumors abounded regarding Mr. Obama's background that his campaign established a Web site to correct the misinformation.

When the *Washington Post* published a piece on the beliefs of some people in Findlay, Ohio, regarding rumors swaying the local vote, Findlay's paper, *The Courier*, reprinted the story, along with local reaction.[17] Understandably embarrassed, the story "In Flag City USA, False Rumors About Obama Are Flying," had been distributed to 669 news organizations in 56 countries, including the local paper.

Without showing partiality for a candidate, which is not lawful for preachers to do in the pulpit, how might preachers develop a sermon about the "Gospel truth," using this example? After reading the story online, do you feel its purpose was to embarrass the people of the town for their alleged gullibility, or was that result a byproduct of a story about the insidiousness of false rumors? Media are reporting how individuals with their own political agendas are producing videos and posting them on the Internet to discredit their preferred candidate's opponents with little financial investment due to the availability of inexpensive software products.[18]

Because we enjoy the freedom in the United States to express our beliefs and say what we like, even if it's "false, provocative or hateful–without legal consequence," we must become more discerning when we are presented with questionable information.[19] Other countries, such as Canada, place limitations on free speech. Some Americans would like to see restrictions placed on hate speech. When I gave a workshop called "Tolerance and the First Amendment," some participants objected to being required to *tolerate* the inflammatory speech of others. What are your thoughts?

Humor and Satire

The reason that humor is used frequently and successfully in advertising is that it catches our attention. Some columnists and commentators use humor and satire as persuasive tools, as do political cartoonists, though they are not necessarily seeking belly laughs. That practice backfired when the Danish newspaper *Jyllands-Posten* published twelve political caricatures of the Prophet Muhammed allegedly to "test whether Muslim fundamentalists had begun affecting the freedom of expression in Denmark."[20]

Many Muslims prohibit even positive visuals of Muhammed both in worship and in secular settings. Violence and condemnation erupted all over the world as some outraged Muslims protested against both the visuals and the negative messages many of them depicted. Even with the passage of time, this issue remains an iconic example (pun intended!) of how humor in one culture may be offensive in another. The complexity of Islamic principles and traditions regarding the creation and use of pictures of any kind, not only in political cartoons, but even photography or clothing patterns, demonstrated how important it is for media producers to acquire the same level of expertise about cultural values and traditions as it is for diplomats.

Humor is used often to defuse difficult situations during press conferences. Guests on news programs or political forums may use humor, sometimes self-deprecating, as they debate their points and counterpoints, creating an environment for persuasion through their affability. As well, when they let their guard down somewhat, their audience perceives them as approachable. Preachers, too, know that a light comment may gain the attention of or refocus their listeners so they will become more receptive to the serious parts of the message.

Integrity: Testimonials and Charisma

Testimonials and charisma are connected with authority figures whose integrity will increase sales or receptivity when they speak on behalf of a policy, product, or issue. Researcher Dr. Robert Jarvik was featured in a television advertisement for Lipitor, a medication that reduces blood cholesterol. Neither a cardiologist nor even a licensed medical doctor, Jarvik, who headed the company that made the famous artificial heart, was representing the Pfizer Pharmaceutical company's product, appearing as an authority, when Congress intervened.[21]

When powerful individuals appear in front of the camera, people listen to them, aware they carry prestige and an aura of celebrity. For example, former Vice President Al Gore has raised considerable awareness of climate change and is one of the most prominent public figures working on behalf of policy changes that will positively affect the environment.

Celebrities such as Bono, Mia Farrow, or Angelina Jolie have been able to accomplish much to raise our consciousness of dire issues in the world via their personal charisma. Their compassion and active witness is often enough to persuade others. When we receive messages where powerful figures endorse products or make policy statements, we may want to ask why we should believe what they have to say. There are several Web sites to consult, including www.Factcheck.org, from the Annenberg Public Policy Center.

The "Big Lie," Repetition and Negative Reinforcement

Most of us really want to believe that we are receiving truth from media sources. To counter the real possibility that information sources are too limited to provide a complete picture of an issue, conscientious media will conduct thorough reporting, even investigative reporting over a long period of time. Too often over the past several decades, we have been disappointed to find that some of our leaders lack integrity. Typically, when "The Big Lie" is detected and confirmed, the press offers no mercy, nor should they. Lying to the media is dangerous for the perpetrator, because integrity is media's most powerful asset, as it is for preachers.[22]

"The Big Lie" begins with an oversimplification that may have a kernel of truth in it. Then it is repeated until it is ingrained and believed completely. The lie perpetuated in negative advertising by the 527 organization of Swift Boat colleagues of John Kerry in the 2004 presidential campaign caused many voters to discredit the candidate's patriotism and war record. The kernel of truth was that some who participated in the advertising actually served with Kerry. Similar tactics were used against Sen. John McCain when he ran for president in 2000.[23] As political ads on television become more mean-spirited, media-literate consumers should deconstruct the messages and see through the persuasive tools that are being used to influence their votes.

Repetition in media, whether repeating lies or facts, is a form of psychological conditioning that may affect consumers. A marketing technique long used by advertisers, more repetition means greater brand name recognition and consumer identification with the product (or story).

When negative elements are repeated, we must be concerned about their impact on consumers of any age. Fictional violence in crime dramas and real violence on television news have conditioned us to accept visuals of brutality and carnage as normative. When television stations aired images from the DVD created by Virginia Tech shooter Cho Seung-Hui, prior to his horrific acts on campus in 2007, many producers had second thoughts some hours later, even though they deliberated extensively about the material they chose for broadcast: "It has value as breaking news," said ABC spokesman Jeffrey Schneider, "but then becomes practically pornographic as it is just repeated ad nauseum."[24] I have observed how repetition affects the elderly, who may become "news junkies" when they are alone too much. They fixate on disturbing stories, watching them over and over, and often become depressed.

Media providers know that negative news fascinates consumers. Crimes, especially murders, scandals, or inappropriate behavior by public figures, including journalists, capture our attention. A spate of racist comments on-air and during public presentations by a comedian, a journalist, and a politician became the focus of much reporting and commentary in early 2007.[25] McCannon writes, "Audiences love it. Our violent, aggressive, sexualized media teaches us from an early age to love to hear dirt."[26]

How might we use that in biblical and contextual preaching? Could we engage our listeners with the intense biblical reporting in 2 Samuel 11–12 about David's murder of Uriah with the same success as media does with reporting tantalizing murder trials? Or would such preaching be manipulative, reinforcing the audience's immunity to the evils of violence?

Diversion

When a situation fails to develop as expected or when a public figure wants to refocus on another matter, the media message may contain the element of diversion. An Associated Press story asserted that the people back home thought Israel's Prime Minister Olmert was taking part in peace talks as a diversion from his personal legal issues.[27] When the Bush administration switched its reason for invading Iraq from eliminating weapons of mass destruction to winning freedom for the Iraqi people, diversion was suspected as reporters discovered that both the British and United States governments relied on unconfirmed intelligence. Media rely on the authority and truth of its sources. If the government misleads or is misled, the media will be, also, unless they confirm the facts they are given.

Another component of diversion the media use is called "card stacking," or selective omission. We use the phrase "stacking the deck" when we merely give the best reasons for doing something. We are susceptible to believing what is presented without checking to see what's been left out. The "diversion" may be away from the side effects, for example, of a medication, or away from a balloon payment on a mortgage with a variable rate. Card-stacking involves deliberately misleading the public, often by telling only a partial truth, as in the Enron Corporation scandal of 2002 or the sub-prime mortgage crisis of 2007–2008, when the financial interests and risks of some created financial chaos and ruin for many.[28]

An offshoot of diversion is the tactic some politicians may use to bring out an opponent's weakness without doing so overtly. It may involve a statement that mentions the opponent's weakness as a non-issue, and denies that it should be an issue, such as a candidate's medical history, age, race, and so on, knowing that its mere mention will trigger special attention and unfair prejudice.

Everyone Agrees

Media messages sometimes depend on "herd" mentality, knowing that those who speak out, such as members of a live studio audience or a protest group, can persuade people watching at home. Related to this is the "bandwagon" mode, which suggests that whatever is dominant in popular culture deserves our attention. Advertisers will tell consumers that "everyone needs one" or "four out of five doctors agree." The bandwagon technique persuades us that we must climb aboard if we are to remain relevant.

Some asked whether this factor caused Americans to lose some perspective in the aftermath of 9/11, when we affirmed our love for the United States with patriotic and religious services and a great display of American flags. Might we ask whether passing the Patriot Act and incarcerating numerous innocent people were an overreaction prompted by the patriotic fervor in the country? How do we respond to such measures as preachers? How do we balance the fears of our parishioners with the assertions of the American Civil Liberties Union and other groups and individuals that this legislation was unconstitutional and unjust? For those who have been persuaded that the ACLU is unpatriotic, how might we help people understand that some organizations have a love for their country that moves them to protect the constitutional rights of all citizens, even when the cause may be unpopular?

An example of a local protest that grew into a bandwagon cause was high property tax rates. A homeowners' movement successfully exercised the right to assemble and speak. However, an unexpected result of jumping on the bandwagon was the unseating of the incumbent mayor, who had nothing to do with setting the property tax rates.[29]

Among other persuasive techniques found in media messages are those comments or pitches designed to sell something to the "typical" American. This hypothetical construct is a plain-speaking, common person, who disdains everything intellectual. Persuasive messages constructed to appeal to the "typical" American play on warm and fuzzy feelings such as nostalgia, especially in markets that are more conservative, such as in the Midwest. Visuals of campaigning politicians often emphasize their family images and show the candidate playing outside with children and pets. These are important techniques for attracting the votes of family people. Important issues and logic are frequently absent from these messages.

The attempt to manipulate the "typical" American is seen in political promises that will ease hardship, such as the intention of

Hillary Clinton to artificially lower the cost for fuel for a time by making oil companies subsidize it from their profits. Even the "typical" Americans saw through the opportunistic ploy that would mean little to their pocketbooks.

Still another approach to appeal to people to get on the bandwagon is through messages that focus on the distribution of information. This isn't necessarily negative, because one of the best objectives of media is to inform. Certain media messages provide significant scientific evidence. Articles about limiting our carbon footprint, healthy nutrition, and safety during bad weather are examples of helpful information that media share with the public to get us "on board" for our well being. Media generally consult experts and produce background pieces to support or refute particular claims when new scientific discoveries become news or when generally accepted theories are challenged, as in the ongoing creationism vs. evolution debate.

Timing

One further persuasive tool is timing, a complex mechanism that has lost some relevance with the 24/7 news cycle which always features "breaking news" on cable networks as headlines crawl across the screen, and as Internet news outlets bring us instant access. But timing is still a consideration for those who want to release their stories when they will make the most impact: government, corporations, entertainers, sports, and reporters in the field. This is where daily newspapers often lose the "big scoop" in favor of electronic media. Broadcasters use the tool of timing to entice viewers with promotional pieces to remain for the newscast or stay through a commercial break with a hint about a weather forecast, a detail about a critical story, or a teaser about the personal life of a celebrity.

We realize by now that the use of language of persuasion is not limited to those who edit the final media message. Everyone who provides information or gives interviews, as well as everyone associated with media, has a subjective point of view, issue, program, or product to sell to others. Media is not neutral. Consumers will decide whether they will be continue to listen and be persuaded by the messages they receive.

Preachers are not neutral either. We bring to the texts our life experiences filled with our particular knowledge, biases, priorities, and preferences. So it is with people who listen to our messages. According to Fred Craddock, listeners have the ultimate freedom and responsibility to decide whether or not to affirm the preacher's message:

If *they* have made the trip, it is *their* conclusion, and the implication for their own situations is not only clear but personally inescapable. Christian responsibilities are not therefore predicated upon the exhortations of a particular minister (who can be replaced!), but on the intrinsic force of the hearer's own reflection.[30]

I believe that preaching is an exciting and creative medium that can be enhanced by the preacher's understanding of media. Preachers who are comfortable taking some of media's persuasive elements and using them in a positive way may be able to enhance communication between themselves and their media-accustomed listeners. Saint Augustine recognized that persuasive tools are available to rhetoricians for both good and bad purposes:

> Since the faculty of eloquence is available for both sides and is of very great service in the enforcing either of wrong or right, why do not good men study to engage it on the side of truth, when bad men use it to obtain the triumph of wicked and worthless causes, and to further injustice and error?[31]

People Hear the Same Message in Different Ways

CORE CONCEPT #3: Different people experience the same media message *differently*.

KEY QUESTION #3: How might different people understand this message differently from the way I understand it?

Filters

Media literacy acknowledges that individuals, whether media consumers or producers, bring cognitive filters to the communication process. Whether we communicate on a one-to-one basis or interpret mass media messages, we carry certain beliefs and understandings with us. Through them we make sense of our experiences. We receive and assimilate information based on our influences from the past, which is reason enough for preachers to be familiar with the backgrounds and local context of their listeners.

Like our listeners, we are not experts in most fields, nor are we objective about most issues. According to the influences on our own formation and the experiences we've had, we are likely to interpret media and preach out of our own biases and prejudices, our personal cognitive filter system. Our listeners receive media messages and respond to them based on their personal cognitive filters, which may be quite different from the preacher's set. Among the factors that influence their response are age, gender, race, cultural background, fluency in English, economic situation, marital status, stability, losses, proximity to and engagement with family, educational background, type of employment, health, quality of interpersonal relationships, travel experience, and political affiliation.

Pastoral preachers realize that listeners can be affected emotionally by the news that disturbs. They also need to be aware that when listeners process the messages they receive, they may form opinions quite different from those of the preacher. Families whose members serve in the armed forces, for example, will be far more sensitive to media messages or preaching that even suggests disagreeing with the government's military policy. While such news stories or the sermon have no intention of denigrating the value of military service, those who are close to people who have been deployed to a war zone may perceive through their filters that such stories are critical of their loved one.

Often it appears that the media treats issues as though there are only two ways of thinking, such as Democrat or Republican, dove or hawk, pro-life or pro-choice, when they may actually involve many points of view based on complex nuances and cognitive filters. Media marketing tries to shape consumers' thinking so that they will fit into specific niches for the purposes of advertising. While bilateral categorizing and labeling is often convenient and probably inevitable, it excludes the less tidy opinions of diverse consumers.[32]

Discovering What Is Included and What Is Omitted

CORE CONCEPT #4: Media have embedded values and points of view.

KEY QUESTIONS #4: What lifestyles, values, and points of view are represented in, or omitted from, this message?

Deconstructing the Story

This core concept and key question encourage us to evaluate news stories from the perspective of their narratives. A narrative describes particular features of a situation, including the key players, events, and actions in a story. When we examine a passage from the Bible that tells a story, we identify characters and their relationships, a setting, motivation, a problem or tension, as well as certain values that are prominent in the culture or situation. Both a biblical narrative and a media narrative will have a structure that introduces us to the story, develops it, and makes conclusions. Just as we are accustomed to do when we exegete scripture, when we process media messages, we should notice the social, political, and economic issues that are represented. Here are some examples of questions we might ask of the content, depending on the story.

- Who holds power?
- Who is suffering?
- What behaviors are described?
- Do we identify with a particular concept or value?
- Are racial or gender stereotypes being promoted?

We can add to the narrative of how a particular media piece came together by asking questions like these:[33]

- Who provided the information for the story?
- What are their biases and perspectives?
- Are they "named" or "unnamed" sources?
- Is there balance that includes a critique of a position on the issue represented in the news story?
- Which questions were neither asked nor answered?
- Was data missing to flesh out the political, social, economic, or historical context?
- If there are quotes, does it seem that something has been abbreviated or taken out of context?
- Is the description of events nuanced so that it can be construed as "partial" or "selective?"

For a more dynamic way of preparing for preaching with a news event, we can capture the information we are seeking about the narrative by arranging it on our own story board. A story board in video pre-production is a series of blocks of space for sketching the story and outlining a sequential overview of the graphic and audio elements. In addition to noting the objective facts of "who," "what," "when," "where," "why," and "how," media-literate preachers may ask questions of the narrative, such as those from this section, and sketch the answers in a format that will provide a fuller picture of the news account.

Why Have the Media Sent Me a Message?

CORE CONCEPT #5: Most media messages are constructed to gain profit and/or power.

KEY QUESTION #5: Why is this message being sent?

Product and Message

Advertising drives commercial media. News stories are tailored to fit around the ads or commercials. Advertisers position their messages with media outlets that promote their values in programming, seeking to attract consumers who fit a certain profile for buying their products.[34] Advertisers also seek good fits and maximum exposure for their contributions to community projects. When major corporations sponsored productions from my arts organization, they did so because what we presented was a fit for their advertising target: the bank that wanted to promote its services to upper income mature adults; the family retailer that wanted to be associated with entertainment for children. Everyone is promoting a message.

When I served as artistic and executive director for a not-for-profit arts organization, I became aware that beyond the typical press release or occasional feature, arts groups that buy advertising regularly with particular media receive more free coverage and publicity, such as feature stories and reviews. While not-for-profits seek "free ink" and hope the press will promote their causes, all stories have a purpose and are related to the profit structure. For example, even when media promote charitable causes by providing space or airtime, they boost their corporate image by demonstrating their support for the community. Everyone profits by their generosity.

The message itself can be the product. If a story stems from a government source, the product is the information the government wants the public to know. If it comes from an institution, it is typically created to enhance the institution's reputation. If it is an editorial or regular column, the consumer is invited to reflect on the writer's opinion.

Messages naturally have an agenda and with the agenda is some form of bias. Messages are constructed in different ways using different angles or approaches. Producers of messages plan carefully when they are selling either a material product or a point of view. Commercials for gas-guzzling vehicles will emphasize positive selling points. A government representative trying to sell the public on privatized plans for Social Security will downplay the risk for citizens to lose their future security in a bear market.

Consumers benefit most when media scrutinize the issues from all sides and don't stop with reprinting press releases. The press is only free when it resists manipulation from commercial sponsors or when media owners either refrain from imposing a political ideology or are completely upfront about their position. While the bottom line for commercial media is sales, the bottom line for a media-literate public is the ability to discern the objective and subjective contents of a news message.

Construction Techniques: News Frames

In this section we'll look at narrative "frames," which are different ways of creating formats for presenting news stories. A variety of frames makes news presentations interesting. When researchers for the Project for Excellence in Journalism and Princeton Survey Research Associates examined the content of several national and regional newspapers, they discovered that newspapers usually produce stories through thirteen different narrative frames or structures.[35] Broadcast media also use these framing devices. In addition to describing the frames, I've provided an example for each used in a news story that you can access online.

1. *A Straight News Account* includes the basics of who, what, when, where, why, and how. It is most often used for briefs, press releases, or other short articles. However, even lengthier stories may use this format, especially when a great deal of information needs to be presented. Accompanying a transcript of a story on the National Public Radio Web site was a lengthy straight news piece in question and answer format that provided information about the implications of the flooding in Illinois and Missouri in June 2008.[36]

2. *A Conflict story* deals with confrontational issues between individuals, individuals and organizations and between organizations. Disappointing news from Zimbabwe revealed the failure of the democratic process when the opposition candidate, Morgan Tsvangirai was forced to withdraw because President Mugabe was threatening violence on his followers and refused to step down.[37]

3. *A Consensus story* finds common points of view or agreement. An example is the resolution passed by the members of the United Nations in 2007 condemning denial of the Holocaust. Iran disassociated itself.[38]

4. *A Conjecture story* focuses on uncertainties or speculation. In an interesting report about the possibility that election machines denied a Congressional candidate her full due, the trial judge declared the case itself was built on speculation and conjecture.[39]

5. *The story unfolds a process or history.* The success story of three Japanese auto manufacturing plants in Indiana is chronicled in a news release from the Japan-America Society of Indiana, which celebrated twenty years of activity with a gala event attended by diplomats and executives.[40]

6. *An Outlook story* places the news item in context with history. The *St. Louis Post-Dispatch* published a story recalling how former Illinois Gov. George Ryan suspended executions because thirteen of those condemned to death were found to have been convicted wrongfully. Before he left office in 2003, Ryan commuted most of the sentences of those remaining on death row to life in prison. The article looks at the history of the issue and the lack of progress the state has made to assure fair trials or abandon the death penalty altogether.[41]

7. *A Horse Race story* tells of winners and losers. David Broder of *The Washington Post* discusses the trivial coverage of campaign stories during the 2008 primaries, saying that the "horse-race" type of coverage dominates (who's ahead in the polls), with policy stories making up only 7 percent, and a look at the candidates' accomplishments at only 2 percent.[42]

8. *A Trend story* reflects on cultural practices, political fads, and fashions. A Gannett News Service story, "Product shrinkage eats into wallets," confirms what many have observed, that familiar packaged foods are being sold in smaller containers, often at the same price as they were before manufacturers began this method of reducing their costs.[43]

9. *A Policy story* discusses its creation and reception. A federal judge struck down an Indiana law restricting the sale of materials with sexual themes because it may impinge on First Amendment rights and is too broad and vague to pass a test of constitutionality. The law as written could have applied potentially to museums and general bookstores, as well as to sellers of pornography.[44]

10. *A Reaction story* highlights the point of view of an important individual who has been part of a news story. A story on the state of education in New York City features the responses of several important people including the mayor, students, parents and teachers to learning and safety in the schools.[45]

11. *A Reality Check* investigates the facts supporting the news events. A *New York Times* article investigated the indicators that demonstrate a weakening economy.[46]

12. *A Wrongdoing Exposed* presents information regarding injustice or an act of wrongdoing. An editorial with the headline, "Holding health hostage, making millions wait," urged dissenting senators to pass the legislation needed to continue the President's Emergency Plan for AIDS Relief (PEPFAR).[47]

13. *A Personality Profile* provides information about a newsmaker.[48] "Nurturing the Arts" profiles three women who mentor young

people in theater, music, and graphic arts organizations in Indianapolis.[49]

The straight news frame accounted for just 16 percent of front-page stories. Most stories are framed using a more interpretive approach:

> The news media have shifted their focus toward lifestyle, celebrity, entertainment, and celebrity crime/scandal and away from government and foreign affairs. An even more pervasive shift moves away from the traditional straight-news accounts and toward a featurized and people-oriented approach to the news. This tends to make the news more thematic and make the journalist more a story teller and mediator than a reporter.[50]

The study found that the frames of horse race, conflict, and injustice, some of the frames used when dealing with disturbing news, occupied 35 percent of the front page and were likely to be placed at the top of the page ("above the fold"), suggesting that these types of stories appeal to readers, compete for their attention, and when placed prominently, are considered the most important stories by the paper.

While stories may be placed on the page or in a broadcast order to attract consumers, they are generated by several other reasons or "triggers." Common triggers for producing stories include:

1. Statement by a government official. Example: Global warming will likely create security concerns with humanitarian disasters.[51]
2. News organization initiative. Example: The *Milwaukee Journal-Sentinel's* investigative team uncovers county pension padding and wins Pulitzer.[52]
3. Preview of an event. Example: charity wine event in Ann Arbor.[53]
4. Release of report or poll. Example: The Pew Forum on Religion and Public Life details religious affiliation of the American public.[54]
5. Analysis or interpretation. Example: Discussion of Iran's nuclear policy.[55]

The study also looked at bias within front-page stories of several U.S. newspapers.[56] The researchers noted that many of the stories revealed characteristic biases grouped around these categories:

1. Protectiveness: inclusive of groups and ideas; or minimizing risks. Example: George Will laments the loss of foreign-born science and engineering Ph.D. recipients to U.S. corporations due to immigration laws.[57]
2. Littleguyism: triumph/failure of the individual over the system; or bias shown in preference for the old ways. Example: Business section shows how teens find little employment in the summer labor market[58]
3. Optimism: perseverance, another chance for the people, supportive of modern technology, anti-establishment, or anti-government. Example: New Jersey restaurant owner hosts North Koreans through efforts to find missing U.S. servicemen who served in Vietnam.[59]
4. Realism: that's the way things are; life is not perfect; we can't keep protecting certain types of people and values. Example: A story confronts the reality of Indiana's poor reading and financial literacy skills.[60]
5. Distrustfulness: almost all are liars and corporate leaders and politicians are greedy.
   Example: The fall of New York Governor Elliot Spitzer, formerly a rigorous prosecutor.[61]
6. Fatalism: negative picture of people failing and a lack of positive change. Example: Do natural disasters change the way aid is delivered?[62]

Becoming more aware of biases in media should not dim our appreciation for journalism. It should help preachers understand that many viewpoints contribute to our perceptions of reality, as well as the perceptions of our listeners. Without realizing it, we may incorporate certain structures and angles in our preaching because we need or want to convey particular ideas. We can deconstruct media messages by analyzing them to make sure we are getting the information we need. Although we may construct our messages because we want our "consumers" to experience the need in their hearts to make changes or take action, it may humble us to remember that they "deconstruct" our messages with others after we have delivered them!

Ideas for Practice

Although I've sprinkled the book with some questions for reflection, here are some concrete suggestions to try out the concepts from this chapter:

- Take a print copy of your newspaper or an online version and determine the framing of several stories.
- Select some stories and "deconstruct" applying the five core concepts and five key questions.
- Ask these questions of some media messages:
  - What facts are presented?
  - What modifiers are used to describe the event?
  - What are the sources for the information?
  - What, if anything, makes you suspicious about the story? Do you perceive any particular biases or agendas?
  - What is the story trying to sell? A point of view? Information? A product? A call for action?
- Turn the tables and take one of your preached messages. Deconstruct your sermon, applying the same process as you would to media messages.

Linking Theological Reflection with News Stories as Preparation for Preaching

Brazilian educator Paulo Freire raised the awareness of the poor by helping them find tools to gain information that would in turn empower them to participate in intellectual dialogue that would lead them to engage in society-changing action steps.[63] As I engaged with the *MediaLit Kit*™, aware that it has a basis in Freire's work, it occurred to me that preparing for preaching and working with the core concepts and questions is similar to the processes liberation theologians use, which are forms of theological reflection.

Both media literacy and liberation theology have developed from grassroots movements, are based on analysis, and are action-oriented. Our process integrates the media literacy skills into our theological reflection as we prepare for preaching when the news disturbs. We gather information about the news that disturbs from several sources. Then we analyze the stories and determine how they are constructed. We reflect and pray with the stories and their implications out of our religious tradition, including our scriptures, ethics, and social justice values. Then we take action by preparing preaching, dealing with the news that disturbs in relation to scripture.

At the beginning of this chapter I suggested that everyone can benefit from becoming more aware of media production and presentation. Preachers have an added responsibility to their congregations to connect the realities of the world as they are expressed in the media with the insights of their religious tradition; after all, preaching is both proclamation and interpretation of God's continuing activity in the world. The media-literate preacher will contribute much to a congregation by incorporating a balanced understanding of the news with spiritual and theological ideas to offer the pastoral word in an ever-changing world.

4

Preacher as Mediator of the News and the Good News

Downstream is where state disaster response officials—surprised by the weekend flash flood—tried to get ahead of the dangerous surge Monday, directing an assortment of felons and farmers, Amish and Mennonites, soldiers and Marines to sandbag sodden levees in southwestern Indiana.[1]

INDIANAPOLIS STAR, JUNE 10, 2008

Part One: Preparing Preacher and Congregation

I grew up near the Atlantic Ocean. My parents always laid in supplies of flashlight batteries, food, and water during the hurricane season. I remember participating in fire and air raid drills at school. Years later when my husband and I moved to the Midwest, we taught our children to call 911, to seek help from neighbors in an emergency, and to go to the basement during tornado warnings.

While most of us make contingency plans to minimize physical threats to our family and property, I have a hunch that most preachers give little thought to preparing listeners for crises that might challenge their faith. This lack of preparation is consistent with the way we do pastoral care, because ministers, much like paramedics, are usually summoned during acute situations. On our busiest days, we do "triage," prioritizing the needs of our people, running from one location to another. Extending the analogy a bit further, our preaching

73

ministry during crises might be compared with practicing medicine in an emergency room, where medical teams try to stabilize patients before the real work of healing can take place.

What would happen if we allocated pulpit time for laying a spiritual foundation that might help listeners cope with unpredictable events? Too often, people who experience loss or other trauma also lose their faith and stop participating in the church community. Crises such as joblessness, illness, or death can threaten the stability of families. While preachers must avoid "template" answers to the serious questions of evil, sin, suffering, and loss, they can teach their listeners to seek support for every type of challenge through the Bible and the teachings of the church, and especially by developing compassionate and spiritually mature lay ministers within the congregation. As part of regular preaching, preachers can provide formation for their listeners that will help them deal with future personal struggles as well as those they will share with the community of faith.

The story of Noah and the flood came up as a lectionary text a few weeks after two major disasters, the tragic cyclone Nargis in Myanmar, and the earthquake in China, both occurring in May 2008. I took the opportunity to talk to our church about how we might prepare ourselves spiritually to respond faithfully should disasters impact us. Serving a rural congregation with many farmers, I suggested that we stock our "spiritual pantry" with "jars" of stories and verses from scripture that we can pull out as we need them. (This message, "Stocking the Spiritual Pantry" is found in appendix E.)

Days after delivering that message, I was helping a family prepare for a funeral. As usual, I asked the family to choose readings and hymns based on what they wanted to say about their loved one as we celebrated his life. Raised in the church and very grounded spiritually, the deceased's daughter was able to name several scriptures and hymns that related to her father's character and also spoke to her whenever she needed consolation. She was accustomed to reaching into the treasure trove she had accumulated from her childhood.

During this same time period, Indiana experienced some of the worst storms in its history, with entire towns under water, major roads collapsing, and enormous economic and property losses for individuals, businesses, and government. No longer were disasters far away. At this point the farmers of my congregation could not count on an adequate harvest in 2008. Coincidentally, in my message the previous Sunday, I had suggested that we carry the theme of "stocking the spiritual pantry" throughout the summer by inviting members to share their stories in the monthly newsletter. A listener ran with my image, suggesting that we set up a pantry in the narthex with jars where people could insert their comments and stories, and that we pair this activity with a food drive for the congregation's pantry. While I had hoped to extend the life of that message, I was happy for the creative input on how to keep the concept of spiritual preparation in front of the congregation.

Preaching beyond the Pulpit

Preaching during worship is just one way we can share the healing Gospel and help our listeners grow spiritually. Perhaps the pulpit could become the catalyst for encouraging members to participate in activities that complement preventative care preaching events: Bible study, special panels and forums, presentations from community resources, Web sites, and reading materials. Ideally, the church will form small groups, where listeners will gather in groups of up to twelve people meeting frequently to pray and learn together through theological reflection and faith sharing. These small church communities will learn to minister to one another during illness or grief, and also share and encourage each other's faith, particularly in times of disturbing news. Members of these groups will learn to become active listeners, both to one another and to the preacher. Do you agree with Samuel Proctor's comment: "Crises do need a quick response, but preaching to community concerns requires also a steady diet of solid, continuous attention to certain priority issues that underlie many of the crisis issues that emerge"?[2]

Preachers who enjoy writing might explore Web-based and print opportunities to offer support and education to the congregation and greater community. Journalists are valuable resources for preachers interested in writing effectively. Thomas Friedman of *The New York Times*, and Leonard Pitts of the *Miami Herald* are two syndicated journalists who bring logic, clarity, and unambiguous positions to their interpretations of news events. I will discuss their work and that of others in chapter 5.

A congregation's Web site can become a powerful tool for Christian education and serve as a place for listeners to provide feedback about issues and sermons. The preacher can facilitate dialogue through a blog that moves listeners out of the role of passive pew-sitters into active collaborators in the ongoing meaning and influence of the message. Taking advantage of technology to evangelize our members and stir up their enthusiasm helps expand and redefine the role of preaching and gives the message a longer lifespan in the community following Sunday worship. Now, with so many more people online, communicating through blogs and podcasts extends the church's reach to visitors and others who may welcome these opportunities to connect with the Gospel and a faith community. Youth and younger adults especially may be receptive to our use of these newer ways of communicating.

Peer Support

As a member of a lectionary group that meets weekly, I grow immensely from the shared wisdom of my colleague ministers as we plumb the Sunday texts. We take turns leading the sessions, distilling the riches of a variety of exegetical and interpretive materials. Our group encourages and assists its members to preach prophetically as we develop and share strategies that address the needs of our congregations.

If travel and time prevent pastors in your community from meeting in person, an online network of preachers could communicate via e-mail as sermons are created, sharing ideas and even asking for examples and stories. With peer support, preachers will likely acquire more confidence to venture into sensitive social justice areas that often become disturbing news. An established network of local preachers could support each other in the midst of community crises and help unite the community.

Getting to Know Our Listeners

Joseph Jeter affirms my concern about the need for faith development before a crisis occurs, even anticipating that crises will occur. He quotes James Oglesby: "When crisis comes ... if you don't have a faith, you don't have time to go out and get one; if you don't have a relationship with your people, it's too late to build one." He echoes my belief that it is a good practice to preach on the theological questions that occur *during* crises *before* a crisis occurs.[3]

As part of a congregation's crisis preparedness program, I suggest that pastors ask every participating member or frequent visitor to provide some basic information that includes legal name, family contacts, family and faith history, educational background, community and church service, interests and anything else they'd like to share. When a member who nobody knew by her legal name was hospitalized, I tried to track her down. Privacy laws prevent information clerks from suggesting alternative names, so it took until evening before I received a call back from a family member. Soon after, I sent out that request for information!

By piecing together the influences that have made them the congregation they are, as well as the seekers with vision we hope they become, we will acquire information that will help us preach more effectively in crises, or when speaking about controversial topics, including biblical justice issues.

Fred Craddock speaks of three ways that ministers might acquire this information: formal, informal, and empathetic.[4] In addition to a formal written questionnaire that many people will complete, preachers will learn the stories of the members of the congregation through conversations during scheduled ministry events, from chance interactions, or during social opportunities with members, as well as through deeper, reflective discussions that probe difficult issues and require much sensitivity from the minister. We also learn a great deal about our members when we visit with them in their homes and in the company of their spouses and children. When we honor the variety of life experiences of our listeners, as well as the collective memory of the congregation, we will discover why people will have different responses to the disturbing news we may discuss in our preaching.

We need to not only get to know our listeners' personal stories, but also to listen to multiple versions of the congregation's narrative, the stories of the joys and crises that have affected the members. The preacher will find it especially helpful to learn about the church's growth or decline, renewal, and transformation. Just as issues occurring in the past may linger and cause concern for individuals, the members of congregations may harbor guilt, resentment, grief, and anger over unresolved issues.

Reaching a Variety of Listeners

Besides becoming familiar with our listeners' personal stories, we will find it helpful to understand the different ways in which they process information. If we want our message to be heard by all, we need to accommodate a wide variety of demographics as well as personality types and learning styles. I was surprised when several adolescents greeted me warmly after worship at a church where I was filling in during Advent and Christmas. Later, I realized that the youth had connected with my sermon, which had focused on the story of Joseph and Mary finding the missing twelve-year old Jesus conversing in the temple with the priests.[5] The church youth had identified with my message about seekers and how adolescents need to separate from parents to find their path, even when some take time off from church along the way.

I wasn't targeting youth in the sermon. I was targeting parents who don't always respond well to this aspect of adolescent development. What this example suggests to me is that when we address a congregation of diverse listeners, we need to be aware that people of different ages, cultures, and genders who have different dominant learning styles and personality factors will receive information and respond to it in different ways. While we are preparing our preaching, we can note along the way who we are including and who we might exclude inadvertently.

We can learn about some of the available materials about diversity, including standard preference evaluators and the differences they measure. For example, while most people measure "E" for extrovert, on the Myers-Briggs Indicator, which means they prefer to take in information from their surroundings, preachers will want to learn how to communicate their message to the quarter of the population who are introverts–those ponderers who mull over the information for a while before responding. Or, using the example of Neuro-Linguistic Programming (NLP), what language can we use to appeal to listeners who perceive their world less through auditory means and more through visual or kinesthetic, hands-on approaches? Demographic factors, such as age, gender, and cultural background will cause our listeners to weigh our messages against their life experience. To add more complexity, even our own personal characteristics will influence the shape and language of our messages.

For example, since many clergy are introverts who often spend a great deal of time in the mental world of ideas, they need to learn how to preach for extroverts by using language and images understood and appreciated by both introverts and extroverts. The woman who took my image of a spiritual pantry and turned it into a concrete activity is an example of relating a message to people who see their world differently than we do. In another situation, someone I know wrote a reflection about attending a church for the first time and seeing a ritual that most attendees would take for granted. He was lifted up as he observed racially and economically diverse worshipers of all ages coming forward to receive Communion together, with hands open, which he felt expressed their need and readiness to be fed with the Bread of Life.[6]

While increasing our ability to connect with a variety of listeners is valuable for preaching in general, it becomes even more critical when preaching during a crisis or when offering faith formation to the community in preparation for a time when disturbing news might affect their spiritual well being.[7] Understanding the demographics of our congregation and providing communication in everyone's "language" are essential to the art of pastoring. For the preacher who wishes to convey messages of hope and consolation, the ability to speak to distinct groups within the membership is vital. A valuable tool for preachers is *One Gospel, Many Ears*, by Joseph Jeter and Ronald Allen, which systematically examines the many demographic factors present in congregations.[8] While it would be difficult to plan preaching to reach every specific group at the same time, preachers will gain significant insights both from understanding how people listen differently and from analyzing the content and diction of their sermons as they learn to change their approach to reach a broader base of the congregation.

To communicate well with different age groups, preachers will choose language that will keep their attention. For example, children, youth, and adults go through certain stages of cognitive and faith development. Preaching a Children's Moment to five-year olds using metaphors won't succeed because what is real to them is what they can see or what they have experienced. For example, when small children saw the destruction of the Twin Towers on 9/11 shown repeatedly on television, they thought the attacks were happening over and over. Preachers will benefit by studying James Fowler's stages of faith to gain insights on the wide spectrum of places their younger and older listeners occupy on their spiritual journeys.[9]

On September 14, 2001, designated the National Day of Prayer and Remembrance, I shared a message with a full church of children and adults who gathered while still in shock and grief over the horrific events that had happened three days earlier. I confronted the terrible reality of the crisis, directing my initial comments toward the older children and adults, but I focused more than half of the message on the younger children, who ranged from six to fourteen years of age, and I was aware that I had to use examples they could understand. The complete text is included as appendix F.

The Challenge of Listener Diversity

We can assume with some certainty that our listeners are at different stages on their faith journeys and that they experience and practice their faith in various ways. Not all listeners are grounded in scripture. Not all pray regularly. Not all have received formal religious education. Perhaps some listeners lack the background to integrate the spiritual and theological implications of Christianity into some of the critical issues of their lives. Several may not have made an association between the gospel imperatives and current justice issues. When the life experiences and general education of the listening audience are very diverse, preachers should take the differences into consideration as they prepare for preaching.

When we become aware of the unique stories of each member, we can identify those who may be carrying burdens from past experiences, as well as those who express extreme political views or biases. Preparing the congregation ahead when planning to preach on sensitive issues may encourage those with differing views to be more open to listening. When preachers assert their role as the congregation's lead teacher, some members may, for the first time, connect reading the gospel with embodying its message. Offering opportunities for feedback and dialogue might encourage listeners to reflect and comment, opening up understandings for listeners and preacher alike. How this is feasible in a particular community is based on the preacher's time and ingenuity, and perhaps availability of technology. In large congregations, this process might involve multiple staff or a team of trained lay members.

I have been fortunate to serve in congregations where most people have appreciated hearing sermons that connect the values proclaimed in the gospel with the challenges we face in the world. Occasionally, some listeners have resisted or resented what I had to say because they haven't had enough background to understand the synergy between today's justice concerns and what Jesus taught his followers about justice. A few years ago, when I spoke about our responsibility to become good stewards of the created world, I mentioned that the United States was not a signatory to the Kyoto Treaty. Some listeners felt that it was inappropriate to imply that the president's policy was incorrect. Others doubted the data on global warming, and some couldn't understand the connection between being good stewards of the earth and the Christian disciple's responsibility. Now, a few years later, after much media attention and public conversation, congregations are more likely to respond favorably to measures that will protect our planet.

In hindsight, I could have been more effective as a preacher if I had prepared my congregation over a period of time to understand both the concept of biblical justice and the disturbing news of global warming. Because it wasn't an emergency, I might have distributed information and held discussions to lay the groundwork for the message. Delaying the preaching until after they had received adequate preparation might have increased receptivity among some listeners.

Also, I should have been more aware of the level of political opposition to environmental laws within that community–a depressed, former General Motors factory town, where factory closures have forced young and even middle-aged workers to find work elsewhere. Those who resisted the message were bitter about what had happened and were still grieving the loss of the flourishing plants they had depended on for economic survival. Now, as rustbelt towns continue to struggle, the governor is working to revive the automotive industry in Indiana, creating partnerships with Japanese carmakers to build hybrid vehicles.[10]

Issues of Church and State

Many people believe that when clergy protest against unjust laws or government policies they are violating the separation of church and state. As I discussed in chapter 1, the "wall of separation" was originally designed to prevent the establishment of a national church and the imposition of religious doctrines on our citizens. Does that mean that the church and its adherents should refrain from responding to justice issues?

In the United States we have the right to speak out against injustice. At times activists may knowingly violate specific laws that result in their being arrested. These people are prompted to engage in civil disobedience by their moral or religious convictions.

John McClure and Burton Cooper discuss how cultural identity may influence the way we live out our religious identity. They constructed five models based on how the church views the world: The Church Against the World: The Ethics of Opposition, The Church with the World: The Ethics of Harmony, The Church above the World: The Ethics of Hierarchy, The Church and the World in Paradox: The Ethics of Dualism, and The Church as Transformer of the World: The Ethics of Conversion. These typologies are helpful in understanding how Christianity can speak with many different voices on major issues, such as war and global economies.[11]

Denominational attitudes as well as social position and economic status may move people to assert their religious convictions and respond to world issues in a variety of ways. Taking this a step further, the way preachers and members of their congregations see the relationship of their church to the world may influence their response to justice issues. One of the most polarizing issues within the United States, as well as in many other countries, is illegal immigration. Many Americans, including practicing Christians, believe that the rule of law is the only consideration when dealing with immigration reform. However, for many pastors and people of faith, the issue is not black and white, and the immigration dilemma requires the mercy of Jesus, not deportation.[12] Supported by their church's tradition of social justice, some groups offer sanctuary in their churches to undocumented workers who are threatened with deportation.

Representing the opposite pole, and quite critical of church leaders who advocate amnesty or other less rigid approaches to immigration reform, CNN's Lou Dobbs is unequivocal that only those here legally should be permitted to remain, arguing articulately for strong government enforcement.[13] A report by Media Matters Action Network suggests that Dobbs and other cable news personalities have devoted a significant amount of programming to reinforce certain negative myths about immigrants that influence their audiences.[14] It's important for us as preachers to realize that the public forms opinions based on media presentations, whether or not the information is accurate.

If we are to live the biblical justice values we preach, church leaders and their congregations may feel compelled to express their views to media or at public forums when policy and Gospel seem to conflict. But since we don't all agree on what the Gospel teaches, preachers shouldn't be surprised at the passion about particular issues within their own congregations.

Which Issues Move Preachers to Speak about the News That Disturbs?

Collections of sermons provide historical evidence of the struggles that captured preachers' interests long ago. In 1933, among the issues that disturbed preachers were prohibition, racial equality and civil rights, communism and socialism, exploitation of people, and capitalism.[15] In 1988, Samuel Proctor named these as chronic crisis issues: family dysfunction, drugs, lack of educational opportunities, and homelessness.[16] Two decades later, the flagging economy, care for the poor, war abroad and terrorism threats, violence and other crime, immigration reform, health care, and environment are some of the major concerns to our security and well-being that may enter into our preaching,

Many preachers often connect their messages to pressing issues. Many others, however, are reluctant to do so because opinions in their congregations are so diverse. Three thousand years ago, the prophets of the Hebrew Bible criticized their political leadership for their shortcomings, predicted that their sinful behaviors would lead to disaster, and insisted on repentance, conversion, and forgiveness. People of today, less familiar with the writings of the prophets, are unaware of how much responsibility was vested in religious leaders to provide moral direction. Courageous preachers can become change agents like the prophets of old. However, as I mentioned earlier, achieving change may require creative advance preparation for some people who might resist the message to really listen and not tune out.

The news that disturbs us may be triggered by a particular crisis of great magnitude, but more often it concerns an issue that has been around a long time and remains unresolved, such as immigration reform or street violence. Like most people, preachers often need significant exposure to disturbing news before being moved to speak out. Most of us may need at least seven encounters before engaging with an issue. (Marketing experts say that we need about seven repetitions of marketing materials over six to twelve months before we make a purchase.[17]) For example, globalization's effect on the poor throughout the world, as well as on workers in the United States who have experienced the outsourcing of their jobs to lower-paid workers abroad, took a long time to penetrate the consciousness of most people. Preachers need time to become familiar with the stories of injustices in the news before they begin to connect them with the Gospel and try to raise the consciousness of their listeners.

Among the ways we can both prepare our congregations and preach on a specific issue that might be controversial is to follow the annual observances that link education with worship possibilities. Among them are Juneteenth, World Refugee Sunday, and Children's Sabbath.[18]

The Liturgical Year as Preparation to Deal with the News That Disturbs

I believe our ability to understand the life and death of Jesus in the context of our lives is a key to our spiritual wholeness. Helping our congregations deal with the complex issues of suffering, death, and the expectation of emerging new life is essential for coping and healing following disturbing or tragic events. Because we are more focused on maintaining our comfort during the good times, we naturally avoid mentioning crises or preparing for the possibility that life will include unpleasant experiences, as well as the death of persons and dreams.

The liturgical year with its seasons that deal with themes of suffering, redemption, and new life provides a foundation for preaching that teaches and prepares a community for difficult times. We need to connect the biblical stories with our personal and congregational stories. The lectionary is actually arranged to help us. Toward the end of the liturgical year around the time we celebrate All Saints, the lectionary readings speak of both the end times and eternal life.

The readings for the first two Sundays of Advent in all three cycles deal with apocalyptic themes, and the entire Advent season is about waiting and longing. Lent and Holy Week provide opportunities to confront loss and grief. With Easter season readings proclaiming new life in Christ, this is an especially good time of year and context in which to celebrate the mystery of healing and growth that will, with God's help, usher in new life and help a person triumph over tragedy or the death of a loved one.[19]

Ronald Rohlheiser names five places within the liturgical year that help define the paschal mystery: "Good Friday, Easter Sunday, the forty days leading up to the Ascension, the Ascension, and Pentecost."[20] He offers solid theological, spiritual, and scriptural texts for the Christian witness of suffering, death, and the receptivity of new life following the experience of death. Whether we are dealing with losses in the congregation or startling world events, this teaching could raise the congregation's awareness about the process of working through significant times of struggle and grief toward renewed life. Rohlheiser offered the following schema to help us understand this cycle so that we could appreciate these events in Jesus' life and in ours.

> Good Friday, "the loss of life–real death"
>
> Easter Sunday, "the reception of new life"
>
> The Forty Days, "a time for readjustment to the new and for grieving the old"
>
> Ascension, "letting go of the old and letting it bless you, the refusal to cling"
>
> Pentecost, "the reception of the new spirit for the new life that one is already living"[21]

The cycle repeats throughout our lives as we undergo many losses and recover from them. Many of these are expected, such as the death of parents due to old age and illness or even job losses in an economic downturn. Tragic events, however, produce a great deal of shock and confusion. Preachers can prepare listeners as a regular part of preaching to understand the connection between events that challenge our faith and the faith of Jesus. The gospels contain many references to death and new life. In his teaching Jesus used familiar symbols and images, such as agrarian symbols of sowing and harvesting, things lost and found, illness and healing. Like Jesus, we can speak of death and healing in images people understand, such as the seasons and special days on the church calendar.

The meaning of special days and seasons in the liturgical year can raise the congregation's consciousness about marginalized people nearby and throughout the world. In the powerful words of Justo and Catherine González:

> We do not have to choose between speaking on Advent and Christmas or on contemporary oppression. A true understanding of the significance of the Incarnation is necessary for a sense of possibility in the present. God is not prevented from bringing in the Kingdom simply because there is not room in our inns…. To become experts at seeing God's manifestations, to be committed to God's authentic mission, these are also part of that (Epiphany) celebration.
>
> Lent takes on a new meaning with a rededication of ourselves to the hard way of the cross that it symbolizes. Even Ash Wednesday could become a new highpoint in a life of discipleship for any congregation. The whole Lenten season with its joining of penitence and expected victory, has strong connections to the lives of oppressors who are themselves powerless, a group that constitutes the congregations of so many of our churches. The culmination of Lent in Good Friday and Easter speaks of the cost of discipleship, the price of sin, and the overwhelming and joyful victory that has actually begun in Jesus' resurrection.
>
> The Ascension points to Jesus' power that continues even now over all other earthly forces and his continued intercession for us. Pentecost celebrates the gift of the Spirit that empowers us and unites us, even in the midst of the present struggle.
>
> To dig to the heart of the meanings of the church's great celebrations is to probe the heart of the gospel itself. In its earliest understanding, when the church needed to hear an authentic, liberating word for itself, it developed these celebrations to remind it of the fullness of the gospel. That word is still liberating for us when we approach it, haunted by the struggles of our time. No superficial celebrations are possible for struggling, faithful Christians.[22]

Preparing listeners to respond to disturbing news from a deeply formed faith requires a great deal of time and energy. But this spiritual formation is integral to our Christian journey as we learn to live within the paschal mystery, which is at the center of our faith tradition.

Part Two: Preaching the News That Disturbs

The Importance of Timing: When Do We Need to Change Our Preaching?

Instinctively, many preachers will feel compelled to address during Sunday worship sudden, distressing news that has occurred within the congregation or local community. Sunday worship is the time when the highest percentage of membership is present. A local natural disaster or human tragedy, the death of a major leader, or an unexpected international news story are all reasons why we might jettison our planned sermon or modify it. It would be impossible for me to ignore dramatic or disturbing news if I knew it was affecting listeners profoundly.

For example, early one dark, snowy December morning in 2003, I turned on the television to check the weather forecast before venturing out to serve as guest preacher for an early worship service. To my surprise the airwaves were filled with the news of Saddam Hussein's capture. As I watched, I considered whether this news would require a major change in my preaching. I decided it posed no threat to the community's well being or need for pastoral care, nor was it an occasion of such magnitude, either positive or negative, that it required much theological reflection from the pulpit.

However, I did feel, on this, the third Sunday in Advent that a brief introductory remark would acknowledge the "elephant in the room" and make a connection between the breaking news and the liturgical theme of joy. I said something like this: "While jubilation may be apparent today in many places in Iraq, true joy will only be experienced in that country if increased stability in the region follows the former president's arrest." Then I moved into my planned message with this bridge: "The experience of true joy illustrated in the first reading from the prophet Zephaniah resulted from God's forgiveness following the repentance and conversion of the people..."

On the other hand, when reports and footage were broadcast showing increasing flooding of rural areas and towns south of Indianapolis, my response was to lift up the victims in prayer and ask the congregation to contribute financially toward their relief. Coincidentally, I had delivered a message about preparing spiritually for natural disasters just two weeks earlier. We updated the call for prayer and material assistance, varying the approach from week to week, offering a slide show that proved once again how photographs convey concretely what words can only try to do.

Big stories like the floods in the Midwest tend to occupy the media for a long time. Reporters cover different angles, such as the personal losses, the response of government agencies, the involvement of volunteers, the factor of insurance claims, and the estimated costs. Sermons can highlight other long-term stories as part of regular planned preaching that informs and may lead to action. These topics include immigration, health insurance coverage, racial and religious intolerance, war, international human rights abuses, water and food shortages, and political crises abroad. Although violent crime, illegal drugs, and poverty are so common in our society, the news might report one situation that has particular poignancy. That narrative could be the centerpiece of a sermon that moves listeners to volunteer with a prevention or assistance program. The same rationale would apply to other areas, such as telling a story of lives affected by rising food costs or other factors in the economy, such as layoffs, bankruptcies, and foreclosures.

When preachers respond to a news event, they will want their listeners to gain some theological insights to apply to their personal faith and discipleship. In addition, the media-literate preacher will help listeners evaluate current information about the news story, amending published inaccuracies or misconceptions as necessary. But above all, when the news that disturbs is very close to the congregation, listeners will be expecting a healing word and encouragement in the midst of chaos. When the news is disturbing, the congregation seeks wisdom and comfort from its media-literate, biblical, and pastoral preacher.

After making a prayerful decision to include the disturbing news in preaching, either immediately or deliberately planned for specific Sundays in the future, an effective way to begin is by reflecting on the assigned Sunday lectionary readings. We may think at first that we will need to change them, but we could be surprised to discover how well the readings of the day provide answers for a particularly difficult situation.

Preaching When Disturbing News Is About Injustice

When media saturate their outlets with a particularly disturbing story, the public, including preachers, take notice. A preacher studying the lectionary passages for the next Sunday, for example, might find a connection between the poor described in the biblical text and the victims described in a media presentation. Or, the preacher might connect the poor on earth with God's freely given love proclaimed in the scriptures.

When Pope Benedict visited Brazil in May 2007, several articles were published about Brazil, the country with the largest Roman Catholic population in the world, which has been a center for the liberation theology movement in Latin America. Despite the Vatican's disapproval of the movement's theology, liberation theology movements continue to thrive with local support. Part of the theological disapproval is over how the liberation theologians see Jesus. They tend to place more emphasis on Jesus as a human liberator serving the poor on earth ("low" Christology) rather than on Jesus, God in heaven, the post-resurrection Christ of faith ("ascending" Christology).

In the reading from the gospel of John 14:23–29, from the lectionary C cycle for the Sixth Sunday in Easter, we hear that God and Jesus will come to dwell in us who demonstrate our love on earth. Coupled with the Acts 16:9–15 text, which describes Paul's encounter with Lydia and her study group in Philippi, we might compare the notion of base communities and bible study groups in Brazil to the study groups of early Church, which were small support communities like those in Brazil that gather to find answers on how to overcome injustice through theological reflection. In my message, I would point out that the poor of Brazil who are seeking answers are God's beloved children in whom God dwells.

While I probably wouldn't focus the entire sermon around the news story, this example could emphasize God's continual activity on earth. Most likely listeners would have heard about the papal visit, so I wouldn't need to provide much explanation to connect it with the biblical passage.

Just as the press in Brazil and elsewhere picked the liberation theology issue as a major theme of their coverage of the pope in 2007, when Pope Benedict visited the United States from April 20–25, 2008, the press focused largely on the clergy sex scandals that rocked the American Catholic Church beginning in 2002. While coverage of this devastating issue has tapered to the occasional item about compensation or cases of additional victims, the widespread abuse of children and teenagers by priests is one of the most disturbing news stories of the new century. During his visit the pope openly declared his sorrow for the injustices, and even prayed with some of the victims, but failed to censure the bishops who failed to remove the pedophile priests from harming more children.

In her online column for the *National Catholic Reporter*, Mary Gail Frawley-O'Dea, a clinical psychologist who treats survivors of childhood sexual abuse, commented that "sexual abuse survivors often have a low tolerance for ambiguity, partial solutions or the gray that characterizes most of life's issues."[23] Often unable to let go of the trauma, they continue to build their identity around it. According to Yale theologian David Kelsey, "A problem with defining personal identity as the subject of horrific events is that it distorts one's identity by binding it to [those events]. The problem lies not so much with the horror as with the pastness. One's future [and present, added by Frawley-O'Dea] are defined by, and so are in bondage to, an event in the past."[24]

The columnist noted that the lack of concrete and just solutions increases the victims' frustration and anger, which continue to delay healing. Should a preacher speak about any of the areas of abuse, such as sexual, domestic, gender, workplace, or children, it is necessary to understand that for a victim, expressing anger and rage are part of the healing process. I was a music minister in a church where abusive priests had served. While I can't recall any pastoral comments from the pulpit, counselors were brought in to assist the people as they grappled with the pedophile priests they had once looked to for spiritual direction.

Everything possible needs to be done to help victims move from their affect of self-blame and shame, anger and railing against the abuser, toward moving forward. I believe preachers can apply this information, as well as these potent, pastoral words, to both traumatized individuals and congregations that have had abusers in their midst.

> Ultimately, healing for any adult survivor requires that the fevered flush of fury be replaced with bittersweet mourning for what can never be. In the end, there is no justice available from anyone for a childhood or adolescence torn asunder by sexual exploitation. In the end, there are no gestures available from the abuser or his enablers that can set things to right. In the end, survivors must fight to heal.[25]

The revelations of sexual misconduct and cover-ups were constantly in the media. However, if I chose to incorporate a less-publicized news report about victims and injustice I might want to challenge the congregation to gather more information, especially when the situation is far from their experience, such as the next example.

Nicholas Kristof wrote a column for *The New York Times* in which he explained how sweatshops have raised the standard of living in Asia and that jobs in them are eagerly sought. Despite his profound and consistent advocacy for justice, Kristof was asking readers to accept sweatshops, even though they exploit women and children, as more desirable than poring over garbage dumps to make a living. Essentially he advocated sweatshops as a preferred form of pragmatic injustice.[26] This column and his later series on the sex slave trade in Asia were extremely disturbing to me. While they raised my consciousness, because the issues are so complex, it might be challenging to use them as illustrations within a typical sermon. However, it would fit well within a *series* of topical sermons connecting the Gospel's theological implications with the many justice concerns regarding industrial globalization.

Confirming Facts and Moving toward Action

When creating awareness about a situation during or prior to preaching, be sure to investigate the news story as fully as you would exegete the scriptural text. Use the media literacy tools described in chapter 3 to analyze the accounts that you hear, view, and read. Since you will be more knowledgeable about the particulars of certain news events than members of the congregation, when speaking with a smaller group or from the pulpit, provide sufficient background and articulate clearly the moral or ethical implications in the news account that motivate you to speak about the issue. Convey why the Christian community is called to learn about disturbing issues as part of their discipleship and to take action if possible. For example, a possible action step to halt the exploitation of children in foreign sweatshops that produce items for consumption in the United States is to boycott or focus attention on the local retailer who sells products from corporations whose overseas contractors exploit their workers. Or conversely, the faith community could actively support retailers and other not-for-profit organizations that sell fair-traded goods from under-developed countries.[27] The prophetic preacher will try to point the way toward equitable solutions to unjust situations and motivate their listeners to do the same.

Prophetic Preaching: Dealing with Evil, Sin, and Suffering

Clearly, evil, sin, and suffering are palpable in the news that disturbs and in the major issues regarding the limitation of human freedom. The preacher's own theology of morality and ethics as applied to these issues determines whether and how these concepts will be presented to listeners. All preachers do not see evil, sin, and suffering in the same way. Although we may define evil as the opposite of that which is good, we may not all agree on what is "good." For example, Mary Jane Trau defines evil as "any thing, act, or state of affairs which destroys the unity of persons or creates circumstances which foster disunity or hatred."[28] Philip Wogamon, on the other hand, defines evil as "anything that obstructs God's ultimate purposes..." He then makes this distinction between sin and evil:

First, all sin is, by definition, evil. But not all evil is an expression of sin. I am thinking especially of natural evil–for example, earthquakes, famines, diseases, unpreventable accidents in which people are hurt or killed before their time or are, in other ways, unable to be what God created them to be… When we neglect to do what we *could* do to alleviate natural evils, that surely is a form of sin![29]

Preaching prophetically requires that we remind people to live the teachings of the Bible, pointing out the values Jesus taught. Certainly, the preacher's task is complicated by the variety of interpretations and nuances about fundamentals. For example, I have discovered that the commandment, "Thou shalt not kill," is translated often as "Thou shalt not murder." The distinction between killing and murdering can influence decisions about the morality of war and capital punishment. Also preachers can be scolded and intimidated by those who prefer that they deal only with personal, not public morality. Roland Leavell tells this story:

> A businessman said to a preacher, "You preachers should stay out of the affairs of the state or nation. Politicians should run the government and preachers should attend to church affairs." The preacher replied, "Then we should tear out of the Bible most of the preaching of the Old Testament prophets."[30]

Preaching with biblical texts demonstrates how episodes of human exploitation in biblical history are comparable to those occurring in today's world. Leavell affirms the role of the preacher as prophet: "A prophet of God should sit as it were on a lookout point and observe everything that degrades or destroys the moral and spiritual life of the people and nation. If there is evil, he should become a troubler and disturber, as was Elijah (1 Kings 18:17)."[31] I have heard preachers say that their role is to "comfort the afflicted and afflict the comfortable."[32] The problem, however, as one of my parishioners pointed out, is that many of our listeners have joined churches later in life and haven't acquired a foundation in the Bible that would expose them to the prophetic books. If that is correct, perhaps preachers might introduce a variety of short sessions about the Bible to encourage further study.

This discussion has covered several bases relating to preaching about disturbing news. We've distinguished a crisis event that threatens the well-being of our listeners from disturbing news reports that reveal injustices. When listeners are unfamiliar with issues or don't have sufficient background to help them identify the issues with biblical justice themes, it's wise to prepare the congregation before preaching on any issue that could cause division. Preparing the congregation for the eventuality of a crisis is important for their future spiritual health. In the next section we examine how preaching in crisis is a vital part of pastoral care.

Pastoral Care and Preaching: Responding to Crisis and Trauma

When people are disturbed by the news they read, hear, or watch, they may be adversely affected, both psychologically and spiritually. Researchers have reported post-traumatic stress reactions not only among those who have survived disasters or violence, but also among those who experience these events *solely* through media coverage:

> Even those who only watched the events unfold on TV may experience strong psychological reactions...People's reactions to violent events with loss of life vary greatly, and there are no correct or incorrect responses. All survivors, including witnesses to the events, even those who only watched it on TV, may experience fear, disbelief, and helplessness in the initial days after the event. Over time they may experience, among other things, feelings of horror, anxiety, depression, and even numbness (lack of feelings).[33]

Post Traumatic Stress Disorder (PTSD) drew significant media attention following the bombing of the federal building in Oklahoma City, with severe incidence higher in females, in those who knew someone hurt or killed, and in those who were influenced by exposure to media coverage.[34] According to the Post Traumatic Stress Disorder Alliance, of an estimated 70 percent of adults who have lived through an experience that could be considered traumatic, up to one-fifth will manifest symptoms of Post Traumatic Stress Disorder. Symptoms described range from re-living the event, avoiding reminders of the event, and being on guard at all times, to psychiatric disorders, self-destructive behaviors, and a host of physical symptoms.[35]

Charles R. Figley, Ph.D., of the Florida State University Traumatology Institute, reflected on the Columbia Space Shuttle tragedy on February 1, 2003, and proposed five questions to ask when we are confronted by disturbing news. Figley suggests:

> "The degree to which we are assured by our answers is the degree to which we can overcome our fears and live a normal and productive life with the full knowledge of the traumatic events we have survived."[36]

The information we gather as we try to answer the questions guides us as we cope with difficult challenges. The five questions are:

- What happened?
- Why did it happen?
- Why did I act as I did (when learning about the tragedy)?
- Why did I continue to be bothered by this (tragedy)?
- Will I be able to cope if something like this happens again?

Figley believes that by itself the Columbia Shuttle tragedy would not have been sufficient to traumatize the public. However, and this is important for preachers and pastoral caregivers:

> It reawakens our general anxiety that has been stimulated by other more personal traumatic events, including 9/11, the economic downturn, and other stressors....
> We need to take stock in what unhealed, emotional wounds we are carrying around...Take the time for soul searching, compare notes with friends and loved ones about what you are feeling and why. Sometimes our faith and spirituality enable us to discover and manage these conflicts. But if these do not work, seek out the help of a professional counselor to address and answer these universal questions of the traumatized.[37]

For those who serve congregations, preaching is an important piece within their overall ministry, which probably includes pastoral care and many other duties. During times of local or national crisis we need to monitor the individuals in our communities who have previously revealed emotional dysfunction, those whose wounds are unhealed, and those who are isolated from the church community because of poor health or by choice. Can we identify those who might be at risk? It's helpful to know how some people might respond during a crisis before one occurs. If a congregation has endured crises with pastors, profound conflicts within the membership, a tragic death, such as a murder, or the destruction of the church building, the informed preacher will be in a better position to help or seek outside help for the congregation, if it is needed.

Pastoral Care and Preaching: Grace and Consolation

Some people attend church services because they thirst for a connection with the Divine and seek direction from a pastoral leader who has the expertise and gift to facilitate that connection. In times of uncertainty and confusion, people come to worship seeking stability, which they expect to find in familiar hymns and rituals. Those who preside over worship and proclaim the Word realize that every act within and surrounding worship has the potential for providing comfort and drawing people closer to God, beginning with hospitality offered at the door of the church until the last person leaves the building. Worship is an aggregate of invitations to grace found in moments of welcome, praise, proclamation, confession, communion, stewardship, education, discipleship, blessing, and mission.

The preacher's message is a vital component among the several invitations to grace. Together with all of the other elements of worship, preaching has potential for filling the well of longing and thirst and opening up possibilities for transforming daily lives. Worship, including the sermon, can serve as a first step in pastoral care and in an ongoing ministry to help heal troubled individuals. The sermon may function for some as a gateway toward healing, bringing together the listener-seeker with the preaching-pastor. As Church of Christ preacher Mark Frost wrote: "For a local church minister, the task of preaching can never be far removed from the congregants' needs for spiritual care…. One of my goals has been to preach in a way that lays a foundation for individual pastoral care."[38]

The following are some suggestions for engaging with listeners in order to lay a foundation for pastoral care:

- Dedicate time to listen to individuals in the congregation so they can express their fear or distress.
- Visit and include those who may be isolated or because they live alone.
- Invite members to assist in the process of healing within the congregation by sharing their experiences of loss and healing.
- Discover the strengths and weaknesses of the community and how members coped in a previous crisis or serious situation.
- Be prepared to converse openly and charitably with listeners who disagree with your position on controversial issues.
- Establish clear reasons why you invite listeners to hear your view of the critical event in terms of the Gospel of Jesus.
- Use additional scriptures to support and illuminate the text you are using for the preaching.
- In times of disturbing news for the community or the greater world, proclaim consoling scripture passages that offer hope of God's love and God's promise to be with us always.

Most preachers are delighted when people discuss what they've heard in the Sunday sermon. Not infrequently, something moves a listener to contact the preacher for guidance, perhaps a word that challenges or inspires hope. In my experience, both the words and the persona of the preacher may encourage a listener to seek personal counseling or spiritual direction. Remember that non-verbal communication is important, too. The preacher's "non-anxious" presence apart from her words must embody that of a calm servant who can be trusted, one who offers compassion and hope, in short, a person you want to have around during a crisis.

The more disturbing the news, the more the message should support listeners' needs for reassurance. Most theological or moral-ethical words can be postponed until listeners have some distance from the event. The sensitive preacher will tell the gathered assembly what she would say to individuals. When the onset of war, sudden violence in the community, or the announcement of the closing of a plant that employs a significant number of residents creates turmoil, preachers are expected to respond with words and rituals that calm the fearful and empower them with courage necessary to go through the difficult times that lie ahead.

Ralph Underwood describes pastoral care as "a ministry of communication with God and people that draws its life from the community of prayer…Pastoral care is nothing if it is not a witness to the presence of God in all conditions of human life."[39] As part of the church's overall ministry of communicating the Gospel, the sermon plays an important role in the pastoral care of the congregation under normal conditions. In crisis the role of pastoral care in worship and especially the sermon as pastoral care becomes a focal point because people look to their pastor to maintain or restore stability during a crisis.

It isn't ever necessary or desirable that preachers mask their feelings completely during a crisis. Honesty with listeners is important because they want to identify with the preacher as both a companion sufferer in time of crisis and as a person who empathizes with the pain of others. Because disturbing news can evoke and stir raw emotions, preachers should be prepared to spend time with those who need to process their feelings.

I believe that it's better to acknowledge that we don't have all the answers and allow for ambiguity and mystery than to speak in theological clichés. When one has nothing more to say, a quiet pastoral presence is a better option than hollow statements like "God had his reasons" or, at the funeral of a young person, "God needs young people in heaven, too." All of us need to learn when speaking is unnecessary and when merely being present serves in lieu of words.

When a tornado ripped through her Alabama church, killing twenty people—including her own daughter—Pastor Kelly Clem was asked all the "why" questions by her members. She realized those questions couldn't be addressed during a crisis. The questions she posed for her congregation as she delivered her Easter message the following week were these: "What am I going to do with the life I have today, with the family members I have today, with the church I have today? How can we be the comforting church when we're all suffering?"[40]

Ideally, the preacher who speaks during crises will prepare messages that are prayerful, healing, sustaining, guiding, and reconciling, messages that contribute to good pastoral care. Listeners will need to be reminded of the power of God's grace that inspires us to continue on even under the most difficult circumstances. All of us want to hear that God loves us and is with us on every step of our journey. People expect that messages will provide direction and lead them forward, like the message preached by Kelly Clem. In the aftermath of a natural disaster or a particularly tragic accident, we will understandably ask where God can be found in the experience. The preacher's responsibility is to help listeners become aware of God's grace in their midst in the present time and to place their situation in perspective.

Authors Ronald Sider and Michael King write about three dimensions of grace and how preachers can make God's grace known. They define "savage" grace as that which we receive when we acknowledge the oppressed and begin to work in different ways to alleviate their pain and improve their situation. We connect with that grace when we confess that we have been complicit in keeping people marginalized because of our inattention and inaction. This grace motivates us to act on our new understandings.

In speaking of "empowering" grace, they tell us that "to preach empowering grace is to share the good news that, in the midst of the painful changes God calls us to consider, God's enabling presence throbs. It means for the preacher and congregation to realize that the more they follow Jesus, the more they will understand what it means to follow Jesus."[41] Empowering grace is found in the surrender we may make to do the will of God in all things, even when the path is difficult. It is the grace of both the oppressed and the privileged, who find themselves together in the net of the Christ, the fisher of people, grasped by a loving God who won't abandon them.

The authors describe "comforting" grace in terms of the congregation's longing to receive God's unconditional love and forgiveness.

For example, when we speak about the plight of oppressed people to listeners who haven't deliberately tried to hurt others, the congregation can become encouraged by learning that despite their past inadvertent passive complicity in political and economic structures that undermine the lives of the oppressed, they can use their gifts from now on to build a better world. Some in our midst may intensify their relationship with the oppressed of the world through their own struggles, victimization (such as domestic or other kinds of abuse, or gender- or age-related marginalization), illness, or disabilities. Preachers can help listeners find comfort and grace in their anxieties, losses, guilt, and the opportunity for new life through telling the stories of how God has comforted the people.

Philip Gulley and James Mulholland tell similar stories in their controversial book, *If Grace Is True: Why God Will Save Every Person.*[42] They boldly proclaim their thesis that God will save everyone, carefully supporting their discussion with a logical examination of scripture. Their work was published as a response to many Christian fundamentalists claiming that salvation from God is a commodity that must be earned. I believe with these pastor-authors that it is important to reassure fearful listeners that God loves all of us unconditionally, especially in this postmodern world of religious pluralism, where within families members may observe several different religious traditions, or feel uncomfortable practicing any of them.

Occasionally when planning funeral services, I find family members are anxious about whether their deceased loved one merited a berth in heaven. Judgmental religious leaders, perhaps persuaded that one must follow certain laws to gain entrance to eternal life, have emphasized rules over grace, often instilling a great deal of fear. In this circumstance as counselors or preachers, we don't need to look further than the story of the Prodigal Son to find our loving parent God who welcomes us home and will always be available to us despite our shortcomings. In difficult times, we call upon scriptures that reveal God's everlasting love and grace outpoured for all to comfort the community and lead its members toward healing.

However, the transformation from grief and anger to forgiveness and reconciliation can only happen over time. Rarely are victims able to offer forgiveness immediately following a crime, nor should they be pressured to do so. Likewise, it is unrealistic to expect people who are in the midst of tragedy or crisis to understand that new life will necessarily follow their loss. Preachers can help people understand that grief work is a process that can't be hurried. The Gospel requires us to love our enemies, to pray for them, and to be reconciled with them, if possible. This is one of the hardest things Jesus asks us to do.

What guidance can we offer to our community of baptized persons who feel anger toward those who commit murder in terrorist attacks, in street violence, or by oppressing populations? The follower of Jesus is invited to overcome the urge for retaliation by bearing witness to Jesus' love and desire for reconciliation. Hard as it is to keep forgiveness and reconciliation in the forefront in the worst of times, these are essential ingredients to living a Christian life and furthering peace in the reign of God. The divisive issue in the United States over maintaining or abolishing the death penalty is an excellent example of this type of challenge to our natural inclination to judge and punish.

Preachers too must be aware of their own affect and avoid angry, arrogant, or anxious language, carefully filtering any biases or prejudices they bring to the preaching task, especially when suffering along with the listeners. As spiritual leaders of the congregation, preacher-pastors are responsible for restoring equilibrium among the people, avoiding responses that might further raise anxiety.

Robert Waznak suggests that preachers view the tradition of preaching as a lament, as naming the pain and revealing the tears.

> There are times when we must not be so anxious to fast-forward to Easter Sunday…We must not be afraid to preach mystery. We do not have the power to end evil, suffering and death. But we do have the grace that comes from the paschal mystery, which invites us to pick up the shattered pieces of our world and make something holy out of them. [43]

In a letter to his congregation, as he extended his pulpit ministry following the shooting rampage at Virginia Tech on April 16, 2007, Rev. Michael Mooty offered these words of hope with suggestions for making something holy out of evil:

> Jesus asked those who followed him to tip the balance. Kindness, compassion, friendship, forgiveness, doing justice, welcoming the stranger, protecting the vulnerable, making peace. What can one person do? Do not ever discount any act, however small, that makes the world a safer, saner, more livable place for someone else. When we do goodness, love kindness, and walk humbly in the midst of our human family, we participate in God's ongoing work of transforming the world into what we call the kingdom of God, a time and place in which all of God's children can live free of fear. [44]

Summary

In this chapter I have described some suggestions for preaching during crises and/or when the news is disturbing. Not everyone becomes disturbed by the same news. Whether we call our decision to speak out prophetic or conscientious, the following points may apply:

1. Become aware of the news behind the headlines. Study world and local issues in the news to find connections between the injustices you see in them and the message of Jesus.
2. While most news events won't prompt a change in the preaching plan, when something serious arises, continue to dialogue with the lectionary passages for that Sunday before seeking other scriptures.
3. Consider forming a lectionary group of preachers meeting in person or online that will become a resource for improving its members' preaching, as well as support during crises.
4. Examine historical collections of sermons that have dealt with the disturbing news of their day.
5. Remember the call to preach the Word of God even when that word is uncomfortable to hear.
6. Incorporate the news in your preaching in different ways. News stories need not dominate a sermon. Rather, they can be used as examples or illustrations to interpret scripture.
7. Controversial situations in the news may require advance preparation for the congregation before preaching.
8. Develop strategies so the preaching will reach all the demographics within the church. Become familiar with some of the inventories that assess personality and learning styles.
9. Grow into the role of the congregation's head teacher. Develop educational and spiritual programs and resources that will connect the people with the world's issues and those of the Gospel.
10. Read and listen to opinion and commentary in print and electronic media. Discover the techniques and patterns of communication that experienced columnists employ.
11. Incorporate the media literacy tools from chapter 3 when evaluating major news.
12. Consider using a Web site and e-mail to extend the life of preached messages, as well as a blog for feedback from listeners and for providing background to news accounts impacting the preaching.

13. Engage members of the congregation to take action to alleviate the suffering of victims described in the news that disturbs that were highlighted in the preaching.

14. Provide preaching and congregational activities that lay the foundation for faith responses for future crises and news that disturbs. Find opportunities throughout the liturgical year to connect the paschal mystery with the natural cycles of human experience.

15. Reflect on the pulpit as a place for group pastoral care and group spiritual direction rather than as a time for theological discourse during a time of crisis.

16. Be honest with your feelings when preaching during a time of disturbing news or crisis, but avoid angry, anxious, or arrogant language even when the news story elicits such feelings.

17. Refrain from stating reasons for a tragic occurrence or using theological clichés.

18. Do emphasize hope for the future and God's covenant of love and presence.

19. Plant seeds for forgiveness and reconciliation as a way of living even during crisis, but don't expect people who have been hurt to move to a stage of forgiveness before there is sufficient time for healing.

20. Review Fowler's stages of development, as well as the principles of developmental psychology. Learn how to communicate with children and youth of different ages, recognizing their limited ability to use metaphors and abstractions.

As I reviewed the above twenty suggestions that summarize this chapter, I realized that most of them focus on the preacher's preparation as a foundation for preaching when the news disturbs. While we can't prevent disturbing events, we can offer spiritual development that will help our listeners cope when personal or community struggles turn their lives upside down.

I believe that in addition to theological studies, preachers will benefit from having a strong foundation in psychology and pastoral care, especially grief counseling. In addition, preaching the news that disturbs requires a degree of media literacy that can be acquired easily by using the information provided in chapter 3. Just as remedying the suffering of the poor was a substantial part of Jesus' ministry, when we pay special attention to news accounts about the poor, marginalized, and underserved populations, we will begin to identify the poor of the gospel with the poor of our time, thereby leading our listeners to respond to their needs.

By engaging with the disturbing news through a wide range of print and electronic media, preachers can become a sacramental voice of compassion in a challenging world. As mediators of the news and the Good News, preachers have the opportunity and authority to lead listeners toward living God's Word through love and grace.

5

What Preachers Can Learn from Journalists

We are surrogates for the American people. Very few places in the world have the kind of protections, particularly the Constitutional protections, we have in this country as a free press. And we have an obligation for all those men and women who work hard all week long in real jobs that when they turn on CNN or turn on NBC, or pick up a newspaper or turn on the radio, they realize that someone else is working as hard as they are trying to get to the truth. And it is not an easy job, but you know what, Larry, it is the best one you could ever have. It is a vocation being in journalism.[1]

TIM RUSSERT (1950–2008)

When NBC's *Meet the Press* host Tim Russert died suddenly on June 13, 2008, shocked journalists, politicians, and viewers mourned this journalist who lived by the highest personal and professional standards of integrity. As NBC chief foreign affairs correspondent Andrea Mitchell said, "He was always teaching each of us to be as rigorous as he was in looking at all the facts, examining everything and then being as balanced and fair and down-the-middle as anyone could possibly be."[2]

Russert, a faithful Christian, easily connected the term *vocation*, often used for ministry, with journalism, which he named as his vocation. Perhaps this helps us understand the vocations of the

103

first-century gospel writers who appeared to function as reporters and commentators on the Christ-Event. They relied on testimonies from witnesses and incorporated stories that had circulated widely. Each author preached to a community of Jesus' followers that had its own particular challenges. That's partly what makes each of the canonical gospels distinctive. Like modern preachers and columnists, the evangelists weren't unbiased or "neutral." They told about Jesus largely through their experience of the oral traditions, the "media" of their culture and literature. Their common goal was to publish the truth about Jesus, to persuade people to "put on Christ," to "imitate God and live in love," (Rom. 13:14 and Eph. 5:1).

Biblical preachers share information and commentary about scripture to assist listeners with making appropriate moral choices within the challenges of daily life. Similarly, one of the most important objectives of journalism is to make sure the public has the information it needs to participate fully in a free society.[3] Since many preachers and opinion journalists deal with moral questions often related to justice issues, I decided to find out what the columnists who address these concerns might contribute to preaching.

I have selected and analyzed columns written by some extraordinary opinion journalists who have taught me valuable skills. I encourage you to read the complete columns from which I've extracted the illustrations. Most are available at the online archives on each publication's Web site or by entering the Web page information given for each column in the endnotes into your browser.

Qualities and Skills

The opinion journalists I admire most demonstrate these qualities:

- A clear sense of purpose or mission
- A desire to reveal and reverse injustice and inequality
- Firsthand experience or extensive research about their topics
- Curiosity to learn about related areas
- Courage to speak what they feel must be said
- Ability to responsibly confront issues and deal with conflict
- Empathy with those who are affected by disturbing news
- Commitment to developing community by interacting with readers or listeners

Many of the skills used by opinion journalists are familiar to preachers. However, the pressures of creating a weekly sermon in the midst of the many additional time-consuming and energy-draining tasks of congregational ministry leave preachers with little time to be creative. Their messages may have less impact on today's media-drenched listeners than they could. Especially when the news disturbs, preachers may want to consider how they can increase the power of their sermons if they hope to move their listeners toward action.

The most powerful sermons I've heard and columns I've read have moved me inwardly toward change or led me toward taking an action step. Often the points gather additional strength because of how the material is presented. Here are some observations:

- Successful columnists are experts in casting their material within riveting stories and imaginative narrative forms.
- They use powerful images, metaphors, and symbols.
- They adapt techniques from television and film, creating vivid scenarios from the objective elements of who, what, when, why, where, and how that capture their readers' attention.
- To keep their writing fresh, they vary the structures of their pieces and frame them in many different ways.
- They use transitions artfully to create movement.
- They write conversationally in clear, precise, and concise language, avoiding jargon, clichés, and unfamiliar vocabulary that would detract from the focus of the column.
- To emphasize an issue that's especially important to them and their constituency, they often plan a series of columns, with separate installments planned to help the reader or listener understand the components of complex issues.
- They use only verifiable facts acquired through firsthand experience and/or scrupulous research.
- They maintain independence from political or corporate influence.

Grounded in Experience and Conscience

Several respected opinion writers have significant academic backgrounds that have prepared them for in-depth reporting on specific topics. Among the most well-known are *New York Times* colleagues Nicholas Kristof, Thomas Friedman, and Paul Krugman.

Nicholas Kristof graduated from Harvard College, studied law at Oxford University, Arabic in Cairo, and Chinese in Taipei. He has lived on four continents, reported from six, and traveled to 120 countries, serving as *Times* correspondent in Hong Kong, Beijing, and Tokyo. He received a second Pulitzer Prize in 2006 for "his graphic, deeply reported columns that, at personal risk, focused attention on genocide in Darfur and that gave voice to the voiceless in other parts of the world."⁴

Following the announcement of Kristof's second Pulitzer award, Jeffrey Brown interviewed Kristof on April 20, 2006, for *The News Hour* on PBS. The columnist discussed his motivation for revealing the immoral events in Darfur:

> ...the idea that we would let Sudan get away with, not only murdering hundreds of thousands of its own people in most atrocious ways, but also to overthrow the government of a neighboring country just strikes me as unconscionable... fundamentally, the reason to act against this is that genocide is something that we can't tolerate in this century... ⁵

Brown recalled a powerful portion of Kristof's column from Easter Sunday 2006: "President Bush and millions of Americans today will celebrate Easter and the end of Holy Week, but where's the piety in reading the Bible while averting one's eyes from genocide?" Kristof's reference to "averting one's eyes from genocide" meant more than turning away and doing nothing. When he travels as a columnist frequently to the same place, he visualizes the people he's met: "...when you put a face on it, then suddenly it becomes a lot more important, and you just feel you have to do something."⁶ Kristof realizes that when he tells the stories of injustices suffered by real individuals, readers become motivated to take action.

Through vivid descriptions of the settings and characters of the places he's visited, Kristof's interviews and reporting put a face on political and economic injustices,. He hopes to inform and imprint his experiences on our consciences as they have left their mark on his. Many preachers come face to face with people who are victims of injustice during the course of their ministry. Could telling their stories make a difference in how the community deals with concerns that were also those of Jesus?

Kristof was the first *Times* columnist to start a blog. Interacting with the public extends the life of the column and creates a following. Short for "web log," blogs may take the form of a daily or weekly journal with postings that are personalized by the individual writer. Readers are invited to reply. Preachers who blog may be building an audience for their messages beyond worship and beyond the congregation. Some have a blogspot on their congregation's Web site. I know from my own experience as a reader that blogs and comments can stimulate concern and even motivate people to take positive action.

Patient Teaching and Precise Writing Using
Effective Transitions

Paul Krugman, recipient of the 2008 Nobel Prize for Economics, was educated at Yale University and MIT and is professor of Economics and International Affairs at Princeton University. His July 30, 2007, column, "An Immoral Philosophy," in which he advocated for health care for uninsured children, caught my attention because I had preached on the topic during my congregation's observance of the Children's Sabbath program of the Children's Defense Fund.[7] Because the State Children's Health Insurance Program (SCHIP) has been so successful in providing care for children with chronic and other health conditions, Krugman questioned the administration's claim that expanding the program would lead to further "federalization" of health care.[8] Krugman concludes that "denying basic health care to children whose parents lack the means to pay for it, simply because you're afraid that success in insuring children might put big government in a good light, is just morally wrong." [9]

While researching his columns, I discovered that Krugman had been dealing with the theme of health care for over two years, not only in his columns, but also in many journals, speeches, and appearances on television and radio.[10] An economist with a conscience, he worked at the problem from financial, historical, and social angles laying a foundation for a wider health care conversation that may lead eventually to universal coverage. Preachers can learn from Krugman's efforts. When convinced that something needs to change, patient teaching about a justice issue through a series of messages may gradually enlarge the listeners' perspective over time as they receive additional information. In addition, when an issue such as health care insurance becomes part of media conversation, preachers can partner with journalists and other voices of conscience, each contributing toward change. Krugman's persistence and the cumulative voices of others have added heft to the national conversation, making health care coverage a priority for the next administration.

Krugman's points are well organized and statistically verifiable. There are no ambiguities. His structure is easy to follow, especially appealing to those who prefer deductive messages. He achieves momentum through ample use of transitions, the "turns" and "moves" with which preachers are familiar.

Preacher Fred Craddock once labeled these transition points, "turns," or changes in direction or a slowing or accelerating of time. He suggested some connecting words to link our thoughts together as though we were connecting scenes in a film:[11]

- "slow turns" (however, and yet)
- "sharp turns" (but, on the other hand)
- "straight stretches" (and)
- "uphill drives" (moreover, in addition, also, beyond this, in fact)
- "arrivals at the top" (so, therefore, now)

Cinematic Structure and Images

Thomas Friedman, foreign affairs columnist for *The New York Times* since 1995, earned a B.A. degree in Mediterranean studies from Brandeis University and a Master of Philosophy degree in Modern Middle East studies from Oxford. Recipient of three Pulitzer prizes, Friedman's previous posts were in Beirut, in Jerusalem as bureau chief, in Washington, D.C. as economic correspondent, and later as chief White House correspondent.

Originally supportive of going to war in Iraq, believing the reports about the existence of stockpiles of weapons of mass destruction in Iraq, Friedman later became critical of the war policy. In addition to his expertise in Middle East affairs, Friedman's additional niche is documenting the developing world and the process of globalization through his books, television documentaries, and newspaper columns.

Friedman sent his column of September 12, 2007, from Dalian, China, where he was attending a conference.[12] He used a familiar postmodern approach often experienced in television and film where the setting shifts from place to place frequently. First, Friedman described his *Sitz im Leben* in China. Then he reflected on America's economic and foreign policies. Next he pondered the war in Iraq, returned to the present in China, and drifted back to Iraq. Despite the appearance of diffused focus on the surface of this column, the theme of "focus" permeated the writing. Friedman noted how China was completely focused on its domestic challenges: economic, political, and environmental. Recognizing that the United States needs to balance national security with pressing domestic needs, Friedman noted that the Iraq War has prevented domestic priorities, such as alternative strategies for energy from developing. On the other hand, Friedman discovered that at the Dalian University of Technology, the current focus is on energy, with 100 doctoral students researching different pieces of energy development.

To underscore what he perceives as misplaced policy focus, Friedman repeated a story he heard two weeks earlier in Baghdad about a unit hit by an I.E.D. Fortunately, because the bomb exploded too soon, no one was hurt, and the soldiers were able to track the detonation wire. A Black Hawk helicopter in the area noticed that someone was taking off on a bicycle. Friedman continues:

> The soldiers asked the Black Hawk for help. It swooped down and used its rotor blades to blow the insurgent off his bicycle, with a giant "whoosh," and the U.S. soldiers captured him... That image of a $6 million high-tech U.S. helicopter with a highly trained pilot blowing an insurgent off his bicycle captures the absurdity of our situation in Iraq. The great Lebanese historian Kamal Salibi said it best: 'Great powers should never get involved in the politics of small tribes.' That is where we are in Iraq. We're wasting our brains. We're wasting our people. We're wasting our future. China is not.

This column illustrates some of the possibilities preachers have for constructing a sermon using an unconventional structure, strong images, and a memorable quote.

Developing Parallel Illustrations to Strengthen a Sermon Thesis

Los Angeles Times Op-Ed. columnist Gregory Rodriguez is a Senior Fellow at the New America Foundation, a non-partisan think tank in Washington D.C. He writes about identity, social cohesion, assimilation, race relations, religion, immigration, ethnicity, demographics, and social and political trends. He is the author of a book about how contemporary Mexican immigration will change the way Americans view race.[13]

In one column Rodriquez responded to the release of Mother Teresa's private letters in which she revealed her doubts and spiritual emptiness over a period of many years. While some writers suggested Mother Teresa's outward religiosity was hypocritical, Rodriquez suggested otherwise by offering his readers a parallel story about Sister Mary Rose. In introducing her, Rodriquez commented, "...it's good to be reminded that those whom many consider saints are complex human beings who more often than not defy convention."[14]

Sister Mary Rose was an American nun who felt compelled to leave Phoenix for Romania to found an orphanage and family assistance organization. From Rodriquez's description, she seems to have shared some of the same strong and sometimes intimidating personality characteristics associated with Mother Teresa. "Brusque, opinionated, hard-headed and not the best listener I've ever met, Sister Mary Rose had an agenda, and I think she viewed mere mortals like myself who crossed her path as either people who could help or hinder her mission." But when Rodriquez saw her with the children, he understood her deep commitment: "She smiled, touched and kissed them...many were confined to their beds, and some had unspeakable deformities the sight of which...instantly made me recoil. Sister Mary Rose had the opposite reaction. She would sit down and hold them, sometimes kissing them on the lips." After describing the character of the woman he got to know, Rodriquez wrote:

> Sister Mary Rose never *told* me that it was her faith in God that gave her the capacity to love these children so fully. For all I know, she may have shared Mother Teresa's doubts... But I do suspect that whether they sensed God's presence or not, it was both women's will to believe, no matter how difficult, in the existence of an ultimate source of goodness that drove them to love so deeply those whom others had abandoned...The dark night of the soul is no reason not to act as if the good can outweigh the bad...

Rodriquez wanted readers to be receptive to his opinion that "saints" are driven to do the work to which they are called whether they experience God's presence or absence. The framing device of explaining Mother Teresa by describing Sister Mary Rose shined more light on the complicated discussion of one's relationship with God and how that affects honoring one's call to ministry.

Using Monologue as a Structural Frame

Miami Herald columnist Leonard Pitts often touches my heart. A 2004 Pulitzer award recipient, Pitts usually focuses on racial or political issues. He is transparent about being a person of faith, as his own response to Mother Teresa's spiritual struggles revealed. His column, "I know He's out there–somewhere," is a monologue, a first person account, during which Pitts sits on his deck in moonlight, wistfully hoping for a dialogue with God, while God silently floats in the swimming pool.[15]

> I sighed my frustration. For a moment, the only sound was the water lapping in the pool. Then I said softly, "You know, sometimes, I think atheists have a point. When you see nothing, when you feel nothing, isn't it logical to conclude it's because there is nothing?" I couldn't bear to look at Him as I said this.
>
> "I think the only reason I don't go with them," I whispered, "is because of all those other times when you do see...

something. When you feel connected to something so vast it defies comprehension. It fills you. It settles you. It gives you peace. And you say to yourself, 'Lord, where did that come from? It couldn't be my imagination, because I couldn't imagine anything so…perfect.'"

Still He Was Silent

Pitts' column the previous week was also a monologue. Called "Message to a young man in detention," it was straight talk to a sixteen-year-old spending time in a South Carolina juvenile detention center after being convicted of assault and battery and disorderly conduct charges.[16] Contrasting with the gentle humor of the reflective piece on faith in the perceived absence of God, Pitts' message to the incarcerated teen was a very serious sermon, albeit without biblical citations. He spoke to him as he had spoken to his now grown sons, "Never satisfy a short-term impulse at the expense of a long-term goal. Never do what feels good in the moment if it's going to cost you something that matters a whole lot more in the end."

When I read the reader comments that were posted following the publication of both columns, it was clear that Pitts has made a difference in the lives of many throughout the United States. With these particular columns he strengthened the faith of those who were troubled by their spiritual doubts, and he gave hope to parents who were struggling with children who were throwing their lives away.

What can preachers learn from his columns? They can ponder a problem using the structure of a monologue or dialogue. They can learn to share personal faith with listeners, talking about the spiritual journey, specifically helping listeners understand how doubts and questions are a normal part of maturing in faith. Reader response to Pitts' columns demonstrates the effectiveness of a blog or other means for feedback to get people involved and to keep important conversations going.

Powerful Subtext

Reading *New York Times* Op-Ed Columnist Bob Herbert's "The Man in the Room,"[17] reminded me of an experience I had while living in Canada years ago. Perhaps because I was a musician, my pastor shared his frustration about singing "Amazing Grace," a hymn beloved by so many Christians. He explained that he not only despised the reference to "wretch" in the first stanza, but he also felt we shouldn't sing a hymn that didn't mention God. The power of metaphor had obviously eluded him, as God is the "amazing grace" of the hymn's text.

There's something similar about Herbert's piece. The metaphor of the unspoken presence of God can also be missed in this parable about holy presence, which is never even remotely referred to in religious terms. Herbert begins, "Who was the tall young man, the quiet guy with the small wire-rimmed glasses, who was spending the entire day, every day, with the badly wounded soldier in room 5711 at the Walter Reed Army Medical Center?" The thread throughout the story is that question about the identity of the visitor. He visits a patient who had been leading a patrol in Baghdad when he was blown up, losing both legs, his left arm and his hearing.

Herbert, a veteran television and print journalist, who specializes in urban affairs, social trends, and politics, wasn't just reporting on the lives of best friends from high school. His was a deeper message, told simply by interspersing dialogue and narration. The story was about giving and receiving, of the presence of God in the relationship of two people who came to exemplify *agape* love. Before his accident, Luis had supported Josh during a bout with cancer. Now Josh was taking his turn being Christ to his friend. "The people at the hospital were always asking, 'Who are you?... And I'd say, 'I'm just his best friend.'" Herbert comments astutely that words can't explain "the value of Josh's constant presence at Luis' bedside." Luis suggests, "I suppose it's the meaning of love...."

It may have been the combination of Luis' tragic ordeal and the spiritual bond between the two young men that moved me to tears. What preachers can take away from this column is the craft to tell stories about human experience within the context of biblical preaching that may not require naming even a single theological point.

Using Irony, Sarcasm, and Satire

When I was a young student in New York City, an English professor left a lasting impression when he announced that in his opinion just about everything can be treated with humor. While most preachers elicit a chuckle from listeners on occasion, and some skillfully weave humor into their messages every week, humor that engages listeners with the disturbing news often involves irony and satire. Irony and satire can be effective when pointing out practices that are inimical with the teachings of Jesus, such as intolerance by Christians or when people in power take advantage of poor or otherwise vulnerable people. Even Paul uses irony in 1 Corinthians 11:17–22 when he chides the people for their behavior when they gather as a community.

Asked where she gets ideas for her columns, Barbara Ehrenreich replied that she writes about issues that make her angry or curious: "My traditional way of dealing with that is humor. Humor actually can be a way of expressing a lot of aggression. I mean, satirical humor. And I used it for years. Nobody wants to hear a rant." Ehrenreich, a social activist and author of fifteen books, comments on disturbing issues for several major publications.[18] Her online column for *The Nation*, "Smashing Capitalism," packed a wallop from its sarcastic opening paragraph through a poignant conclusion.[19] She wrote about the irony of how exploitation of the poor in the mortgage and credit industries backfired, creating the financial crisis of the second half of 2007.

> Somewhere in the Hamptons a high-roller is cursing his cleaning lady and shaking his fists at the lawn guys. The American poor, who are usually tactful enough to remain invisible to the multi-millionaire class, suddenly leaped onto the scene and started smashing the global financial system. Incredibly enough, this may be the first case in history in which the downtrodden manage to bring down an unfair economic system without going to the trouble of a revolution.

Just as Ehrenreich discussed how the rich have brought this particular crisis on themselves through their exploitation of the poor, a preacher might compare exploitation of the poor in the Bible with examples of exploitation today. Ehrenreich skillfully articulates issues with clarity and humor, issuing a strong indictment against those who fail to hear the cry of the poor, noting that, in the end, despite the effects on the powerful, the poor still suffer at the hands of the powerful. She concludes:

> Global capitalism will survive the current credit crisis; already, the government has rushed in to sooth the feverish markets. But in the long term, a system that depends on extracting every last cent from the poor cannot hope for a healthy prognosis. Who would have thought that foreclosures in Stockton and Cleveland would roil the markets of London and Shanghai? The poor have risen up and spoken; only it sounds less like a shout of protest than a low, strangled, cry of pain.

Leaving Space for Listeners to Ponder

Peggy Noonan is a contributing editor and columnist for the weekend edition of *The Wall Street Journal*. She taught journalism and worked at CBS News before serving in the administrations of President Ronald Reagan and Vice President George H. W. Bush. What I appreciate most in her writing is when she works all sides of an issue, leaving some room for the reader to add thoughts or ponder the choices she offers.

Because illegal immigration has become an issue provoking great controversy in the United States, columnists have tackled it from political, social, and economic angles. Even seemingly less significant, though related topics, such as whether English must be designated the only official language of the United States, can spark heated argument.

In her column "We Need to Talk," Noonan relates an encounter that occurred (ironically) on the Fourth of July.[20] When most workers in New York City were enjoying the day off, a Latina woman was handing out advertisements for men's suits at the major intersection of Lexington and 59th Street in front of Bloomingdale's. After passing by, Noonan went back to offer a word of encouragement and discovered the woman didn't understand what Noonan was saying. Noonan reports that she jotted down these words, "We must speak the same language so we can hearten each other."

Noonan vividly describes the setting, the physical appearance of the young woman, and the nature of the work she was doing. Because Noonan had wanted to be helpful, she was frustrated when she couldn't communicate. In a very respectful way, Noonan opines why immigrants should learn to speak English, while keeping their first language as well. She is against designating both English and Spanish as official languages:

> In the future, with the terrible problems we face, we are going to need to understand each other more and more, better and better. We're going to need to know how to say, "This way" and "Let me help" and "stop" and "Here." We're going to have to negotiate our way through a lot of challenges, some dramatic, some immediate, and it will make it all the harder, all the more impossible-seeming, if we can't even take each other's meaning, and be understood.

However, that's not the end of the story, for she believes Americans should learn additional languages: "We live in the world, and we want that world to understand us better. We want to understand it better, too…For us, at least the older of us, learning another language is still a leap. As a nation we probably should leap more."

The last line addresses a fundamental issue in the conflict over immigration–resistance to change. Often preachers feel they need to tie up all the loose ends, but that can inhibit the listener's natural instinct to think about what was said. Noonan permitted me "to contribute" my thoughts. When she does this within her columns, even though I may not agree with what she says, she leaves room for dialogue. How might preachers keep listeners who have diverse backgrounds and understandings about justice issues involved by a similar bit of "hemming and hawing" that could lead to further reflection?

Persuasion through Education

Although incorrect or debatable facts inevitably infiltrate journalism and preaching–and consumers will need to do their own fact-checking–columnists and preachers of integrity will try to publish only verifiable information.[21] Persuasive discourse is successful when readers or listeners trust the person giving the message. Factual, as well as emotional, arguments can convince people to change their minds and take action.

Anna Quindlen received a Pulitzer Prize for commentary in 1992 while a columnist at *The New York Times*. Author of several books of fiction and non-fiction, Quindlen generally focuses on social issues in her bi-weekly *Newsweek Magazine* column. Like the preacher who sees the Sunday message as an opportunity to integrate the spiritual and secular, Quindlen seeks to integrate world concerns with our personal lives to understand how we fit into that world. In "America Needs its Newcomers," Quindlen used statistics to persuade readers that both documented and undocumented workers are necessary to the economy of the United States, a position confirmed in statements by local, national and corporate leaders.[22] Her numbers show that immigrants compose 15 percent of workers, including one in four farm workers, that Latinos are involved in new business startups at three times the national average, that they often do two or three jobs that go unfilled by others at low wages, that they pay taxes, as well as use medical and educational services. Setting aside the economic argument Quindlen observes, "Immigration is never about today, always about tomorrow." She views productivity as more important than work visas reminding readers that immigrants have traditionally worked hard, eventually employing others.

Would this column have persuaded the people in towns such as Hazelton, Pennsylvania, or Riverside, New Jersey, who were troubled about the impact of illegal immigration to reconsider their ordinances designed to restrict the freedom of undocumented newcomers?[23] Perhaps not. But it does lay the groundwork for dealing with conflict using reason and information instead of fear. This is vital when preaching about disturbing and controversial issues, including immigration. Immigration will continue to be a major social and theological concern for the church. The values of Jesus' gospel about welcoming strangers and caring for them seem strangely dissonant with those for whom the laws are more important than compassion. Preachers serve both God and people of all persuasions when they provide factual information and spiritual direction that will create an environment for further discussion and will diffuse intolerance.

Preaching when the news disturbs requires many things from those who are entrusted with the responsibility of preaching God's word. In addition to spiritual maturity, compassion, knowledge of scripture and tradition, I believe that preachers will benefit from studying the art and craft of journalism, even networking with journalists to replace the news that disturbs with justice and compassion.

6

Behind the Scenes of the First "Preaching When the News Disturbs" Workshop

While researching this book, I was fortunate to be able to test its major concepts with a group of eight men and women using an interactive format. Participants identified disturbing issues in the news, related them to preaching the gospel, worked with media literacy tools, explored strategies for preaching when the news disturbs, and developed a preaching plan using lectionary texts and real situations of disturbing news. It was a privilege for me to be part of this wisdom community and gain much from their comments and insights.

Participants included two male seminarians from Christian Theological Seminary in Indianapolis, where I conducted the workshop. Among the three clergy were two Christian Church (Disciples of Christ) ministers, including a female pastoral counselor and a semi-retired male church history professor, who served for many years as the denomination's chief ecumenical officer.

Two Roman Catholic preachers participated, including a priest who had left the active ministry to marry. He was serving a largely African-American Catholic parish that had refused to merge with another parish when the archdiocese closed their parish and sold its building. The other Catholic participant, a public speaker, preacher, and author, after concluding a business career had returned to school to begin a new vocation as a pastoral associate and business manager. Rounding out the group were a journalist who gives retreats in spirituality for her Methodist church community and a marriage counselor who attends an Assembly of God congregation.

The four women and four men ranged in age from mid-twenties to mid-seventies. Among their undergraduate majors were business, history, education, laboratory science, and peace studies. Although I had designed the workshop with an emphasis on theology as it relates to the news and news media, all the participants enriched the discussion as they drew in their diverse life experiences, educational backgrounds, and vocational choices.

Following the workshop, the participants encouraged me to offer programs for a variety of audiences, including seminarians, clergy continuing education, and special meetings or convocations of denominations. They suggested also that I hold sessions for lay preachers and training for licensed ministers. Since then, I've received additional feedback from laypersons who find the subject appealing and have said they would welcome opportunities to learn about the news and media literacy and how the news relates to biblical justice.

Although I knew at the outset that a full day workshop would be more comprehensive, I scheduled a morning program as an initial step. While a full day would have provided time to prepare and present preaching, much was accomplished with this motivated group of learners. The session included five activities that focused on the highlights of my book.

Activity #1: Defining Terms

We began by discussing the notion of "disturbing news" to arrive at a group consensus of the term. While everyone offered examples of disturbing news, our journalist/workshop facilitator participant created a working definition: "Disturbing news is that which serves as a catalyst for promoting highly-charged emotional dialogue, anger, grief, despair, and mainly difficult emotions." The participants agreed that negative and difficult emotions could result after receiving disturbing news.

When one of the seminarians asked about the possibility that positive emotions could also be a response to disturbing news, he raised the event of the capture of Saddam Hussein reported in the news on Sunday morning, December 14, 2003. The seminarian wanted us to consider that particular news event as "news that disturbs" because he had a difficult time addressing it. Noting that he doesn't usually watch the news or listen to the radio on a regular basis, he told us that he heard about the capture of the former dictator from two people before he arrived at church that morning, because those people relayed the news they'd received from television and radio. (This news event and its aftermath saturated the news. It was important for me to hear how these participants experienced the event, especially in light of my own experience of preaching, which I've discussed in chapter 4.)

The journalist-workshop facilitator noted that she was in Puerto Rico at the time of Saddam Hussein's capture and that televisions in the hotel lobby were showing the clip of his medical exam over and over while the people attending her conference were dancing. The emotion was intense. She suggested that the news of his capture was "important to everybody somehow."

After everyone had contributed their thoughts on disturbing news and the emotions it can evoke, I offered my definition from chapter 1. There I had defined disturbing news as "an event or analysis of an event or situation that may be violent, unjust, destabilizing, inhumane, uncharitable, including all actions or intentions that harm people and the environment, or conflict with the moral and ethical teachings of Jesus." I explained that I included natural disasters and accidents in that definition, as well as acute crises or chronic issues that are difficult to resolve, noting that much disturbing news deals with humans devaluing other humans, depriving them of freedom, limiting their choices, and preventing them from living fully. Participants readily offered examples, including several relating to liberation theologies, such as the chronic political crisis in Haiti, Israeli-Palestinian conflict, and same-gender marriages.

The pastoral counselor reflected how some news that should disturb doesn't disturb. Drawing upon her background as a laboratory technician prior to her theological studies and subsequent ordination, she used an analogy dealing with the way things are held in tension. Describing the surface of water, she suggested that something needs to disturb or disrupt the surface to break the tension of its smooth surface. The news that disturbs thus breaks through the surface of both the media and our consciousness causing a first "plunk" and then ripples outward.

As we moved into defining the term media literacy, I asked the participants how they receive their news. They mentioned *The Indianapolis Star*, radio, television, and the Internet. Several listen to National Public Radio, and others consult *The Washington Post, Common Dreams, Daily Grist*, Michael Moore's Web site, and My Lycos. One woman differentiated between two of our local Indianapolis television newscasts, claiming she watched one of them to get the straight news and the other for a folksy interpretation of the news. While the latter station's news held the highest ratings, it was now leading with the most sensational local story, in contrast to two of the other stations, which place those stories later in the newscast. One of our participants told us he restricts his newsgathering to the evening news on television and an occasional glance at the Internet during the day, while several others said they keep up with news as it unfolds during the day.

The seminarian who majored in peace studies as an undergraduate told us that he is very critical of the media. He said he doesn't even like the sources he uses, including the BBC online, NPR, and *The Indianapolis Star*. He consults them to find out what people in the congregation he serves as a student associate minister might be reading or hearing and to discover which issues are in front of his parishioners. Others commented about their distrust of media to provide factual information. Their concern about finding truth in media would form the basis of our discussion in Activity #3.

Activity #2: Looking at Examples of News That Disturbs

As a hands-on learner, I am very well aware that we spend a great deal of instructional time as passive listeners. For that reason, I wanted to offer some different learning styles during the workshop. I provided highlighting markers for the participants and handed them several editions of the main section of *The Indianapolis Star*. I invited them to circle the headlines of stories dealing with disturbing news. This was to establish that much of the news is disturbing news. I had purposefully conceived of this activity for "hands-on" learners to provide an opportunity for those with this predominant learning style.

Although I provided several tables and encouraged everyone to spread out the newspapers, all of the participants chose to stay in our U-shaped seminar grouping. One person stood in her place and was very involved and vocal while she did the exercise, but the person who sat beside her never even picked up the highlighting pen. When I reviewed the evaluation forms, where I had included a question about preferred learning style, (aural, visual, or kinesthetic), only two people selected kinesthetic or "hands-on" as their particular learning style, which explained, (perhaps along with the early-morning hour), why they stayed in their original places. Most of the participants preferred to learn by listening, which was evident as they listened and responded so carefully to me and to one another.

Activity #3: Developing Media Literacy

We were prepared now to focus on media and media literacy. I gave an overview of how news presentations evolved in the media, from brief newscasts to analysis programs such as *60 Minutes,* which tended to replace documentaries with a format of longer segments that could hold the attention of the viewers for fifteen minutes at a time. We talked about the role of documentaries, such as PBS's *Frontline,* which capture a smaller share of the viewing market. One participant thought that the original expectation for magazine format shows was to provide in-depth analysis that would result in balanced facts and opinion. Another commented that the downside of these programs was that the financial success of *60 Minutes* spawned similar programs because they had the potential to make money. The participants observed that the introduction of the profit motive into news presentations led networks to obtain lucrative advertising sponsorships and fashion the programming so it would appeal to a wider public. This, in turn, led toward a tendency to cover more entertainment and sensational news instead of critical news.

We explored the core concepts and key questions of media literacy described in chapter 3. With handouts that assisted the flow of a rather intense discussion, we examined the elements of a media message and each core concept with its accompanying key question. The group quickly grasped the complexity of mass media messages.

To illustrate the issues raised by the core concepts and key questions, the participants were asked to name recent disturbing news events and tell the stories. They selected current events that had impressed them, including the account of human embryos being cloned in South Korea and the suicide of a college student who had volunteered for a prescription drug trial through Eli Lilly, an Indianapolis-based pharmaceutical company.

Here are the core concepts and key questions from the Center for Media Literacy, followed by the discussion starters I created for the workshop:

CORE CONCEPT #1: All media messages are *constructed.*

KEY QUESTION #1: Who created this message?

DISCUSSION STARTER: Since media messages are constructs, many factors influence the development of the presentation. What are they?

CORE CONCEPT #2: Media messages are constructed using a creative language with its own rules.

KEY QUESTION #2: What creative techniques are used to attract my attention?

DISCUSSION STARTER: Remembering that language is more than words, how do media persuade consumers with words, images, music, silence, vocabulary, and camera work?

CORE CONCEPT #3: Different people experience the same media message differently.

KEY QUESTION #3: How might different people understand this message differently from the way I understand it?

DISCUSSION STARTER: People with different experiences will view or hear a message from their perspective. They will also fill in blanks, hearing or seeing what they think they should. Demographics also determine how we receive a message. For example, California fruit growers hear news about immigrants quite differently than do St. Louis shoppers.

CORE CONCEPT #4: Media have embedded values and points of view.

KEY QUESTION #4: What lifestyles, values, and points of view are represented in, or omitted from, this message?

DISCUSSION STARTER: Often news programs or media companies may have editorial positions that influence their publications. For example, many people claim Fox News presents information and stories in a much more straightforward manner than do other networks.

CORE CONCEPT #5: Most media messages are constructed to gain profit and/or power.

KEY QUESTION #5: Why is this message being sent?

DISCUSSION STARTER: Who is supposed to benefit from the message? How?

The core concepts and key questions prompted a discussion of the notorious episode when Janet Jackson's breast had been exposed briefly during the Super Bowl's halftime entertainment.[1] The media message pertaining to the *news* event of the halftime show during the Super Bowl was received on several levels. The workshop participants realized that many people contributed to constructing the message of the actual performance, as well as to the news story that developed out of it. The creative techniques were largely non-verbal, building to the moment when Janet Jackson's clothing was ripped off. This was preceded by the ensemble's erotic dance movements and commercials that workshop participants agreed were unsuitable for the general audience. The group concurred that while some viewers would have found the presentations acceptable, family audiences experienced the media messages differently.

In the aftermath of the halftime performance—which had received huge media attention—workshop participants felt the media were telling them what to think and feel about the event. The group concurred that the exposure of Janet Jackson's breast was not the total story, but that the act of ripping clothes off, which demonstrated sexually aggressive behavior, and the half-time show's theme about stripping, were the metamessage. Referring to the fifth core concept, the participants saw the event as a sales promotion for Janet Jackson's new album, which was also reported in later media coverage. One participant was irate that the networks would make the decision to put subsequent live programming on a one-minute delay, that they took the liberty to make that decision, putting themselves in the role of censors.[2]

The group turned next to two medical stories, beginning with the human cloning account from South Korea. Recalling the media attention given previously to the bogus claim by the Raelians that they had cloned three babies,[3] the participants questioned the veracity of the news account of this scientific breakthrough reported in South Korea, where allegedly a new stem cell line had been formed from cloning a human embryo.[4] The participants noted that the recent news releases stressed the health benefits of the research breakthrough and avoided any ethical judgments. Follow up-stories to the report emphasized how patients with Parkinson's disease were hopeful about receiving treatment with embryonic stem cells. Individuals in the group spoke to the moral questions of both cloning humans from embryos and discarding human embryos. Participants agreed that media are capable of presenting all views. However, individual stories, especially interviews, tend to offer the views of the stakeholders, in this case the researchers and patients.

In the midst of this discussion, one participant, a longtime social activist, questioned the outcome when news outlets are bought out and media corporations merge. He was concerned that with fewer media outlets the opportunity to hear different perspectives becomes less likely, especially since media corporations appear to insert their particular editorial views. He cited the FCC rulings that permitted media corporations to own more outlets, an ongoing concern, which I discussed in chapter 2. Participants felt that consumers should be careful about believing what they receive from media. Some believed that many people do "swallow the news as truth" from whatever source they receive it, without understanding the motivations behind the message. This is, of course, a reason for everyone to become media literate!

The third story that the participants raised during this activity was the tragic death by suicide of a college student who was taking part in a prescription drug trial for Eli Lilly and Company.[5] This story evoked strong emotions within the group. We discussed how college students frequently engage in drug trials to help with expenses. One seminarian compared the practice with an actual apocalyptic comic book story in which people could sell the rest of their lives to pay off debts or assure the future prosperity of their children so that rich people could extend theirs.

The pharmaceutical company was quick to say that its drug could not have prompted the suicide. Because other patients in the study—previously diagnosed with depression—had also committed suicide, participants commented that a media consumer might determine that the company was looking after its assets. They also suggested another perspective, that the media might slant the information to make it seem that the company was at fault. I pointed out that while it is tempting to "bash" the media, in the interest of the truth, media-literate consumers should continue to seek out more information.

Our businessman/preacher commented, "Coming from a business background, I am wary of the immediate leap that if it's big business it has to be corrupt. Who has linked the suicide with the drug? The assumption is there in the headlines."

The pastoral counselor followed up, "It is in the power of media to influence perspective, and we as consumers of information will choose to read the headline and think we know enough. It takes a lot of time and energy to ferret out the truth."

The retired seminary professor offered this insight:

> We learn so much about the abuse of information that we can become jaundiced where we disbelieve everything or suspect unethical behavior by everybody. If we're not careful, we become purveyors of the wrong gospel. And a part of this is becoming totally surrounded by the media and not equally surrounded by the gospel question. Then our preaching becomes just an alternative to the newspapers. And we become excellent experts on all these technicalities, but we don't have a message.

In concluding this segment, I affirmed his summary statement and suggested that our role is not to preach the news, but to preach the Gospel!

Activity #4: Developing Strategies for Preaching When the News Disturbs

While we could have continued the lively conversation about media literacy, we moved to the fourth activity, a discussion of some of the twenty suggestions for preaching when the news disturbs, which I summarized at the conclusion of chapter 4. I invited the participants to choose suggestions they wanted to focus on and to share any of their experiences that might be helpful to the group.

After selecting eight of the suggestions, we began with the recommendation about forming a support group of preachers, both for improving preaching and to serve as companions and resources for each other during crises. The marriage counselor shared her positive experience in forming a support group of Hispanic pastors who were able to encourage each other and offer mutual assistance to parishioners in crisis.

When someone asked about a group process to prepare and evaluate preaching, I described "Partners in Preaching," which I first experienced through my doctoral work at the Aquinas Institute of Theology in St. Louis.[6] First, the preacher and a small group of listeners from the faith community reflect together on the lectionary readings for the following Sunday. Then the preacher may choose to incorporate some of the ideas within the preaching. After the preaching has taken place, the original group or another group of listeners gathers without the preacher present to evaluate the preaching. Then, that group shares a recording or their written comments with the preacher. I suggested that this was a wonderful way to listen to members of the congregation when preparing to incorporate disturbing news, not to mention how beneficial it is to receive input and evaluation from a group of parishioners.

The next preaching suggestion we tackled was that of considering factors of diversity and demographics. This was prompted by a seminarian's comment about needing to reach people of different demographic groups. He believed that even when it appears that listeners share the same views, someone is always left out or marginalized by the dominant conversation. Our activist/married priest suggested that the problems we see in the news are the result of not living the Gospel. Another participant commented that even within communities where the people seem to share the same characteristics, there are differences in how people listen and how their individual experience as Christians informs what they actually hear the preacher say in the message. He also suggested that cultural and faith experiences encompass more than we realize, noting that people "listen" to our manner more than the content or words we speak. The participants agreed that body language or non-verbal communication conveys a large portion of our message. One participant reminded us of the wry comment attributed to St. Francis of Assisi, "When preaching, only use words if necessary." The journalist, who also offers workshops on spirituality, added that our personal spirituality is revealed through both our non-verbal and verbal communication.

The senior member of the group picked up on the suggestion that we avoid angry, anxious, or arrogant language in our preaching even when the news story may elicit such a response. "In prophetic preaching," he said, "it is easy to let it very quickly be known that we have the gospel truth, that it hasn't been in this sanctuary for a long time, and that I have come personally to give it to you." He views this as an example of how preachers can misunderstand their role. During his forty years as an itinerant preacher, he had to reflect on what it meant to break open the word of God to strangers listening to a stranger. He came to realize that preachers can be as much a part of the problem of communicating the Gospel as they can be effective carriers of the Gospel. Another participant suggested that when the ego steps aside, our spirit is open and God's word can come through us.

The conversation turned to the suggestions that deal with giving pastoral care from the pulpit. Participants shared their experiences of preaching or listening to preaching in time of crisis. One man spoke of preaching a homily for the funeral of his former administrative assistant, who died well into her nineties. The family was distraught, and he wished that there could have been time for dialogue to interact with the people during his pastoral and faith-affirming sermon. He identified a need for listening to the people as they were struggling with death and resurrection. Following the homily, he was able to elicit some responses to what they had heard by asking the mourners to recall a memory or shared experience with the woman whose life they were celebrating.

One woman recalled a tragedy when a local pastor, his wife, and their three children were killed after the parsonage caught fire, allegedly because the congregation had neglected to fix faulty wiring. The minister who presided at the memorial service stepped out of the pulpit for the time of preaching to symbolize that he was sharing the crisis together with the community. The participant who shared the story remarked how this gesture resonated with her because she realized that it is tempting for a preacher to stay just outside the crisis and speak *about* the crisis. When the memorial service for this family was held during the Christmas season for a large gathering of mourners, she appreciated that the preacher declined to offer theological answers.

This account reminded a participant who had served a parish in southern Indiana about another Christmas season tragedy, when a bridge collapsed over the Ohio River, killing many shoppers. He suggested that preachers give listeners permission to grieve and be sad, without proposing answers. "In this way, when you say you don't have answers, you let God be God." The group agreed, adding that offering hope was essential throughout the acute process of crisis and loss.

Activity #5: Creating a Sermon Incorporating the News That Disturbs

The objective of the concluding activity was to incorporate information from the first two hours of the workshop and prepare a sermon outline that would include a disturbing news account. To facilitate this practical outcome, I provided the participants with the readings from the Revised Common Lectionary for the First Sunday in Lent, Cycle C, and commentaries for all four readings gleaned from several sources. I offered the group a scenario and reflection questions to assist the small-group process.

Scenario for Preaching Outline

As preachers and involved members of the human community, and as members of the Body of Christ, we are affected by events that take place around us. While we may not all be "disturbed" by the same information that we receive through the media, we are called to consider the events around us and respond, however we choose, as Jesus taught us.

For today's preaching assignment, based on the readings for the First Sunday in Lent, Revised Common Lectionary, Cycle C, we will incorporate the media accounts of a worldwide hunger for freedom— freedom from terror, freedom from domination, freedom to realize hopes and dreams for one's family. Among the news accounts that disturb me greatly are those coming out of Haiti and Israel-Palestine. Haiti is "celebrating" two hundred years of democracy in 2004. Israel and Palestine continue to behave in old patterns, preventing a real peace to take root. The readings during Lent often focus on freedom. How might we pull this together as we prepare to preach on February 29, the First Sunday in Lent?

Reflection Questions:

1. What is it about this news that moves me to respond to it from the pulpit?
2. What do I hear in the lectionary texts for this weekend?
3. How do the texts help me to process the disturbing news, as well as potentially meet the needs of the congregation?

4. What else might I draw into this preaching event: the liturgical season, sacraments? visuals? symbols?
5. What word of faith can I offer to my listeners from my experience, from scripture, and/or from the witness of others?

I envisioned that the participants would initially read and reflect on the four lections by themselves, then engage in a mind-mapping exercise where we would amass all of the participants' first thoughts about the texts on the chalkboard before studying the commentaries. Given the luxury of a few more hours, after the period of individual reflection and the group mind-mapping exercise, I would divide participants into teams to study the readings and commentaries, and ask each team to present their exegesis and interpretations of one of the readings. As a group, we would select a text or texts for preaching through consensus, develop a thesis statement, and suggest structures and strategies, perhaps offering illustrations or examples. This would form the basis of the preaching outline. With extended time, each participant would prepare preaching and receive written feedback.

Since our limited time precluded such a thorough process, I kept the participants together and modified the procedure. The group read the lections to themselves, and individuals offered their "first-naiveté"– their initial thoughts and feelings about the readings in relation to the issue of human freedom. In a very short period of time the chalkboard was filled with concepts and images from all four readings that illustrated the relationship between the texts and the impingement of human freedom. Through their excellent work, the participants realized how preachers can still use the Sunday lectionary passages when the news disturbs without needing to substitute readings. Every suggestion and contribution was significant toward building a sermon on freedom. While one of the participants provided an outline with examples very quickly, all were able to listen to the scriptures and receive insights for preaching guided by the questions I had provided. Through this exercise they also experienced how creative and powerful a group preaching process can be.

Evaluation and Considerations for the Future

I have written this behind-the-scenes evaluation so that readers will understand how rewarding it can be to talk about the issues in the book with a group. Clearly, the material came alive through the described activities and discussions, and I was pleased that the topic stimulated much in-depth conversation. I will enjoy opportunities for leading workshops and discussions in the future, and I encourage my readers to share the ideas in the book with others by developing forums or other activities for their students, colleagues, or members of congregations. Many people I've spoken with want to respond appropriately to the news that disturbs and learn how to understand the media messages they receive.

I was grateful for the excellent rapport and collaborative spirit among the workshop participants. Half of the people attended because they heard about the workshop and found the topic appealing. The others responded when I extended personal invitations. Afterwards when I spoke with a participant who often facilitates clergy support groups and workshops, she commented that although she herself would welcome a full-day workshop, clergy are often so protective of their time that they decline opportunities for continuing education. Personally, I believe that most clergy are very interested in learning more skills for preaching and for other dimensions of ministry. However, the enormous energy required to sustain a pastoral ministry can be so overwhelming at times that clergy (and I include myself), often need *unstructured* time for rest and stress reduction more than an additional commitment.

That said, I believe we should continue to offer opportunities to strengthen preaching and all other areas of pastoral ministry. Because preachers typically prepare for preaching in isolation, many may not realize how getting together with others can enliven their preaching. When they only hear themselves preach, which is often the case for sole pastors, they miss out on hearing how creatively preachers may communicate the Gospel. In addition, whether it's a group of preachers meeting regularly to prepare for Sunday or an occasional workshop, interacting with others can encourage colleagues to deal with tough issues that require careful reflection and attention, such as the many manifestations of the news that disturbs.

Suggesting a structure for a longer workshop, the same colleague reminded me that to cover as much as we did with a larger group of participants would require another hour. For a more comprehensive workshop she recommended two half days or a morning and evening or even two days. I agreed with her assessment that doing activities #1-4 in the first session and concentrating on activity #5 in the second would be optimum. Additional sessions would accommodate listening to the individual preachers, dividing the group as necessary for a large number of participants.

While three of the participants thought that the three-hour session was too brief to assimilate the information, five said it was a good amount of time for an introduction, and five indicated they would benefit even more from a full day. The consensus was that the workshop provided a good introduction and they would like to spend more time on the topic. I pass these comments along so that readers can benefit from my experience as they plan for using the information in the classroom or in special programs.

Some Final Thoughts

If I were to broaden the scope of the workshop on preaching when the news disturbs, I would consider including a segment on how to access quality news and analysis online. Because the Internet has become a tremendous tool for gaining knowledge quickly and efficiently, I would also call attention to a variety of reputable and diverse bloggers who add to our perspective of global issues. If I were teaching a course, I would assign specific television news programs and online news sources and have the students apply the media literacy tools to the messages.

Entirely beyond the scope of workshops for preachers– dreaming on a bigger scale–I would consider holding a conference for preachers and journalists that would include not only sessions dealing with preaching, but also panels, seminars, and dialogues to bring preachers and mass media professionals together. We have so much to learn from each other in the quest for truth and greater understanding.

Several individuals with proven expertise and experience in both media and ministry would be invited to speak on topics such as Media Literacy for Preachers, Civil Religion and Media, Liberation Theology in the Twenty-first Century, Christianity and Culture, Religious Pluralism for Preachers and Journalists, Developing Relationships between Media and Faith-based Organizations, Spiritual Care for Journalists, and How to Avoid Cynicism: Keeping Hope Alive When the News Disturbs. I can envision the Center for Media Literacy in Santa Monica, California, and other such organizations becoming involved by developing print and Internet materials to assist preachers as they assess the news and prepare their sermons.

I hope the ideas presented in this book will stimulate further inquiry and reflection. In times of peace and abundance, as well as during crises or when the news disturbs, God sets before preachers a tremendous responsibility to encourage all who listen to live as bearers of hope and love. What that means to me is that we must affirm what is good and confront attitudes and conditions that are contrary to the gospel. I conclude by leaving you with these questions for reflection. May they lead you to preach boldly and courageously, moving your listeners to action when the news disturbs.

- How might we affirm news media when they report accurate and in-depth information that contributes to our understanding? How do we imagine responding when media coverage is inaccurate or inadequate?
- How might we strengthen the influence of the pulpit as a force for biblical justice while affirming the separation of church and state?
- How might preachers assist members of their congregations to discover the simple tools of media literacy, and how might that make a difference in their understanding of the media and the news?
- How might preachers sharpen their focus on inequities and injustices so that listeners will develop the motivation to confront the status quo, where necessary, and become agents for creating systemic change?
- How does one preach on news that disturbs when one has no answer to the problems the disturbing events raise?

APPENDIX A

The Roots of Today's Disturbing News and the Implications for Preaching

This material provides background information for some of the persistent disturbing news of today. Human struggles involving oppression and injustice are frequently covered by news media. Many of these stem from responses to national and group human rights movements, which include specific liberation theologies that develop to help create positive changes. In addition, I will discuss environmental degradation, the downside of globalization and the rise of radical Islam, each of these issues rooted in the past and affecting today's disturbing news.

Regional Liberation Struggles and Theological Responses

Liberation theologies have developed in geographic regions where oppressed people have formed supportive communities and distinctive methodologies to build faith while dealing with oppression. While the umbrella phenomenon of Latin American Liberation Theology was the first to attract worldwide attention, Africans and Asians have also developed strong theological responses to the suffering of their people.

When bishops met in Medellín, Colombia, in 1968, they proclaimed a "preferential option for the poor" for the work of the Catholic Church in Latin America. Activist priests guided liberation movements by developing basic Christian communities, small groups of caring church members that motivated the laity theologically and liturgically. Among the earliest liberation theologians were Fathers Gustavo Gutiérrez, Juan Luis Segundo, Jon Sobrino and Leonardo Boff, whose writings greatly influenced late twentieth-century theology.[1]

They empowered laypeople with no seminary training to appropriate scripture and interpret it in light of their experience, although government leaders considered their meetings subversive and Vatican theologians consistently criticized the movement's borrowings from Marxist-Socialist ideology.[2] However, for activists trying to solve the immense economic problems in the region, politics and religion are inseparable.

The model of theological reflection, "See-Judge-Act" of Spanish Jesuit Jon Sobrino, who has ministered mainly in El Salvador, begins with the experiences of the people, moves toward reflection and analysis, and then towards committed action. The hermeneutical objective was to understand the relationship between the Word of God and the world through the experiences of the poor. When the poor study the Bible, God is not revealed as neutral, but instead as having a preferential option for the poor.

Brazilian Paulo Freire (d. 1999), who helped to expand liberation theology's focus on ethics, wrote that the poor have knowledge and a way of sharing reality that can lead themselves and those of us who are the advantaged "others" toward "*conscientization.*"[3] No longer kept in ignorance, the poor are supported by the methodologies developed in their particular context that call for liberation. For Freire, the process included raising the consciousness of the poor, focusing their attention on acquiring the facts about their situation and becoming critical thinkers. This process prepared the people for dialogue about systemic contradictions in their society, particularly those contradictions within the structures that limited them. Media literacy owes a great deal to Freire's work.

The "Hermeneutic Circle," a construct employed by Thomas L. Schubeck, S.J., in *Liberation Ethics*, was based on the work of Uruguayan Juan Segundo, S.J. From an initial "ideological suspicion," that something is unjust, this process of theological reflection investigates the background to that structural reality that limits or marginalizes and seeks an interface with theology. The next phase questions the way the Bible has been interpreted in light of the power structure. Then, the fourth step is to discover a "new hermeneutics," reading the Bible from the liberating perspective, based on the work of the people as they begin to understand their situation. This may result in a new and changed ideology, with a praxis or path of action that empowers the people in their struggle.[4]

While Pope Benedict XVI prepared to visit Brazil in May 2007, an article in *The New York Times* noted that 80,000 "base communities" and nearly one million "Bible circles" are doing liberation theology at this time in Brazil. While the movement may be less visible because the hierarchy in Latin America is much less involved, this grass roots movement remains vital.[5]

Liberation theologies in Africa are more complex because the continent of Africa is home to so many different tribes and religious customs. Although colonial missionaries attempted to eliminate ancestor religions, these continue to exist alongside Christianity, with Jesus cast as a "Proto-Ancestor."[6] Today's African Christian theologians, such as I. B. Idowu, seek to make the African church a local Christian institution, not a branch of a European religion as it was organized under colonial rule. Among the many concerns of African liberation theologies are the mistreatment and inequality of women, racism, particularly in South Africa, issues of genocide and intertribal warfare, and the effects of multi-national corporations on land use and local economies.[7] Muslim and Christian tensions often impact on human rights situations, particularly when Muslim leadership administers its own faith-based justice system as it does in parts of Nigeria.[8]

Asian theologies of liberation reflect the diversity of the continent's several major religions that support the faith journeys of millions of people. With Christians accounting for only 3 percent of the Asian population, (including the heavily Christian Philippines), Asian liberation theologies incorporate the perspectives of Buddhism, Taoism, Hinduism, and Islam, among other religions, including Christianity. Wishing to discard European and United States cultural domination and the legacies of colonialism, Asian liberation theologies reject "...the one-way teacher approach which has so deeply infected the Western attitude toward the Third World."[9] The religious response to local oppression is based on creating *indigenous* ways of communicating faith, by contextualizing scriptures and worship to meet the needs of people from the local culture.[10]

Non-Christians have incorporated principles of liberation theology within their faith traditions to move their people beyond restrictive and oppressive political and economic systems. Even before the birth of the Latin American liberation theology movements, Mohandas Gandhi embodied principles of faith in service to the poor during India's independence movement. Women's liberation movements in Islamic and Hindu countries continue to employ the sacred texts and doctrines of their faiths in their quest for equality and justice.

Some Christian theologians have realized that the depth of religious experience and wisdom found in Asian religions and their theologies of liberation can inform Christians, also.[11] Raimundo Pannikar, a Catholic theologian of comparative religion, who lived in India for many years, expressed the need for accepting religious pluralism, writing how, in his opinion, "each [religion] represents the whole of human experience in a concrete way...the dilemma of exclusivism or inclusivism may be solved in favor of a healthy pluralism of religions that in no way dilutes the particular contribution of each human tradition."[12] This position encourages the prospect of bringing diverse theologians and people of faith together to work jointly for freedom.[13] As a Pew Forum on Religion and Public Life study of 2007 reveals, the people in the pew in the United States are already accepting of diverse religious traditions.[14]

Liberation Theologies of Gender, Race, and Sexuality

As women's liberation movements sprang up in the 1970s, a North American feminist liberation theology began with white, middle-class women who resisted patriarchal structures that denied women equal opportunities. Women questioned the traditional interpretations of biblical passages dealing with women or the status of women. Feminist theologians expanded prayer language to recover and include feminine images of the Divine, promoting inclusive public worship language, as well as inclusive language revisions of biblical and ritual texts. African American women, such as Womanist theologian Jacquelyn Grant, pointed to cultural differences that distinguish them from white women, claiming that their need for liberation derives from the experience of being controlled by both male and female masters, even long after the end of the Civil War. Women throughout the world have been influenced by the feminist movement within the United States, and organizations promoting women's rights and equal opportunities have begun to raise awareness of subjugated and abused women in many underdeveloped countries.

James Cone developed a theology of liberation based on the experience of African American men. All his books contain no-nonsense, dialectical writing on systematic theology and the black experience, as he reflects on the work of Rev. Dr. Martin Luther King Jr. and Malcolm X and the major disturbing issues of racism, poverty, and sexism. Writing in the preface to the 1997 edition of *God of the Oppressed,* he said:

> I still regard the Bible as an important source of my theological reflections, but not the starting point. The black experience and the Bible together in dialectical tension serve as my point of departure today and yesterday. The order is significant. I am *black* first—and everything else comes after that. This means I read the Bible through the lens of a black tradition of struggle and not as the objective Word of God. The Bible

therefore is one witness to God's empowering presence in human affairs, along with other important testimonies.[15]

Heavily influenced by Cone's work, Rev. Jeremiah Wright, former pastor of Africentristic Trinity United Church of Christ in Chicago, reminded his community of its African identity: "We are descendants of Africa, not England... "We have a culture that is African in origin–not European. The Bible we preach from came from a culture that was not English or European."[16] Again we identify a unifying thread, the thread in freedom struggles to become free from the historical domination by cultures that habitually deprived people of their human rights. The vibrant urban church headed by Rev. Wright grew its membership and outreach under his leadership. Barack Obama and his family worshiped there until 2008, when the pastor's comments to the press led him to disassociate himself from his former pastor and the congregation.[17]

Hispanic Liberation Theology or Latino/a Theology seeks the experience of faith within the culture and daily life of the people, incorporating a theological process that moves from reflection to faith in action toward a hopeful future. As Spanish-speaking immigrants to the United States struggle to create stability in a country that often fails to appreciate them, a liberation theology emerges from their challenges. Rapid growth of Hispanics in the United States has exacerbated numerous tensions. Adding to these tensions is the government's inability so far to control illegal immigration or implement a fair and realistic immigration policy. At odds with each other are those who would offer sanctuary to those estimated twelve million immigrants who have been living and working in the U.S. without legal documents and those who would deport all illegal immigrants regardless of their work history or that they reside with their American-born children.

Because immigrants from Latin American countries are often racially-mixed descendants of European Spaniards, Africans and indigenous Americans, this liberation theology predictably deals with racial equality, as well as identifying themselves as pilgrims who have fled oppression in their native lands. Biblical themes of inclusion and the stories of journeys of ancient peoples seeking acceptance will assist preachers who want to reflect on the disturbing news surrounding the United States' immigration quandary.

For gays and lesbians, discrimination based on sexual orientation makes headlines as they challenge churches in their pursuit of acceptance both as members and clergy, as well as the legal system in their pursuit of civil rights, including the right to marry. Richard Cleavers reflects on scriptural passages that assist with the process of gay identity, coming out, inclusion in church, especially in ritual celebrations, and most of all the Eucharist. He writes about the gay and lesbian sacramental theology that includes liturgy, symbol, and celebration.[18]

The process of gay partners' attaining the legal rights and protections of marriage has accelerated as various states recognize civil unions or marriages between same-sex partners. Some Christian denominations support the unions of gay couples. Others have dropped their ban on ordaining gay and lesbian ministers.[19]

Liberating the Earth from Human Degradation

After decades of denial, we begin to understand that humans have subjected the planet's health to the same factors that have birthed a variety of geo-political liberation theologies: arrogant dominance over resources, thoughtless disregard for the future, scientific ignorance, greed via destruction of habitats, over-use of land, extinction of wildlife, and poisoning of the atmosphere. We are finally realizing the consequences of our "carbon footprint" and are awakening to the necessity of living "green."

Justice issues are involved in the use of resources, the exploitation of people, and the non-sustainable economies that undermine populations. While replacement of renewable resources, such as forests, can balance their loss, industry has both knowingly and unknowingly seized the riches of the planet and caused incalculable harm to air, water, soil, and forests. Environmental theologian Thomas Berry suggested that the natural world needs to become "a functioning community of mutually supporting life systems within which the human must discover its proper role."[20]

Many of us believe the earth is composed of several interconnected eco-systems and are hopeful that by uniting people all over the world we will reclaim the planet from environmental abuse. Although Christian theology focuses on the worship of the one God, some biblical passages and interpretations stress our need to overcome physicality in order to become more spiritual. Such theological interpretation tended to disconnect the earth (God in nature) from the heavenly (God as Ruler). When the development of industry shifted populations from rural to urban life, many people lost their connection with nature. Noting how *bodiliness* has always been problematic in Christianity, Sallie McFague speaks to this duality in her analogy of God's caring relation to the world and to the way we relate to our bodies: "To love bodies, then, is to love not what is opposed to spirit but what is one with it—which the world as God's body fully expresses."[21]

Another notion that has subverted the care of the earth has been so-called "millennial thinking," whose adherents believe that God's power as ruler will prevail over earthly concerns. McFague criticizes this monarchical model of God for it distances God from God's creation, implies a lack of involvement with non-human life, and encourages people to abdicate responsibility for the needs of the physical world.

A liberating theology re-orienting us to our role in the continuity of the earth will require theologians to perhaps recontextualize Pauline anthropology and environmentalists to influence the means of reversing harmful environmental trends. Celebrating the interconnectedness of life motivated Thomas Berry to formulate his dozen principles.[22] Mary Catherine Hilkert, O.P., who articulates a passion for finding God in all things and all things in relation to God explores this in her theology of "liberating grace":

> Beyond their critical work, feminist and ecological theologians are embracing the most fundamental theological task: exploring and articulating the interconnectedness of all of creation in relation to the mystery of God...find[ing] real affinities with the sacramental imagination's emphasis on the goodness of creation and the body; the location of revelation in creation, history, and human experience; the creation of human beings in the 'image of God'; the importance of incarnation and divinization as well as redemption; the mediation of grace through human persons and communities; the central role of ritual and symbols in human and Christian life; and the essential connections between liturgy and life.
>
> Suffering, injustice, and the "groaning of all creation" are stark realities, indeed the starting point, for liberation theologians.... But together with Hispanic/Latino, African-American, and other forms of liberation theology, feminist and ecological theologies broaden as well as concretize the basic focus of the sacramental imagination on "liberating grace."[23]

Globalization in Brief

Globalization is one of the world's greatest challenges to justice. While the positive effects of globalization potentially include wider interconnectedness and sharing in the world's economy and culture, the negative results from globalization include all of the motivating factors that have encouraged liberation movements to flourish –marginalization of people because of gender, ethnicity, or sexual orientation; destruction of ecosystems and waste of resources; geopolitical movements particular to locales, regions or continents, and economics.

The historical-geographical roots of globalization began in ancient times, when rulers planned expeditions to obtain real and imagined resources in their quest to dominate the world. From the fifteenth century, European powers explored and exploited new territories and resources, imposing cultural and religious structures that suppressed the rights of indigenous people. When British colonial powers, for example, expanded their markets, they appropriated land and resources and created British zones of influence, where the British model of government and society transformed indigenous cultures. After the Civil War, the United States entered the expansionist movement, both in the western part of North America and abroad.[24]

The unification of European nations contributed to expansionism in the late nineteenth century, while at the same time, the writings of Karl Marx began to influence disenfranchised citizens in Europe and abroad. During the first quarter of the twentieth century, economies rose and fell on many themes and variations based on capitalism and socialism, as the radical communist model took root in Russia, and Germany plunged into the economic depression that led to World War II.

After World War II, as the Cold War polarized the world into East and West, non-aligned Third World countries became attractive economic spheres of influence for the commercial interests of eastern and western powers. Over the next few decades, some nations, such as South Korea, were capitalized by the United States and developed new technologies that caused their economies to soar. Privatization became the political-economic model adopted in the United Kingdom under Margaret Thatcher and in the United States under Ronald Reagan in the 1980s. As governments loosened regulations, the policy of privatization enabled private national and multinational corporations to gain control of economies.[25]

When the Socialist experiment of the Bolsheviks failed in 1988-89, with the collapse of infrastructures in the Eastern bloc, the former puppet regimes of the USSR were invited to participate in the capitalistic world. Since then, transnational corporations have influenced much of the economy and politics throughout the world.

Along with government deregulation and privatization, serious problems associated with globalization have emerged, including the end of many small enterprises, family farms, independent stores, and even multiple daily city newspapers. Oil consumption drives many political decisions, including the location for military engagements, while the World Bank decides the fate of poor countries regarding loans and debt repayment. Those nations and corporations that control resources, money, and power shape the world's economy. Planet Earth is often referred to as a global village because rapid travel and instant communication have become the norm. However, these advances have also permitted businesses to engage in corporate colonialism by utilizing and often exploiting workers throughout the world, far away from the company's home base. Liberation theologies will continue to play a role as people seek freedom from oppression and empowerment for workers in this age of globalization. With frequent mergers of large corporations in almost every industry, greater wealth, profits, and power are distributed to fewer people and businesses. As it did in the age of exploration, freedom and justice take a back seat to profit. For example, as multinational oil companies have forged agreements with political leaders in the Middle East, displaced populations in Africa, such as animists and Christians from southern and eastern Sudan, have been forced to migrate north where they face discrimination by the Muslim majority.[26]

Although the global marketplace promises a utopia of unimpeded flow of goods and services, in reality this marketplace is controlled by corporations, governments, and consumers. Poor people and poor countries remain vulnerable. While the idea of a global "just in time" assembly line (getting the right part at the right time to the right location) was encouraging, low wages and below-standard working conditions often prevail because of intense competition within third world countries for factories where major corporations outsource manufacturing.[27] Although globalization was seen as an opportunity to help women in developing countries gain status, women still experience job and wage discrimination and remain tied to domestic responsibilities, as well as their poor-paying jobs.[28] Nations like Haiti with high debt and limited resources find it difficult to share in the global market and benefit from it.[29]

Control of media by a few large multinationals can lead to limited exchange of ideas and cultural exchanges. Clearly, even some print and electronic news media outlets can be perceived as victims of globalization, since they are managed more and more by large, profit-driven corporations.[30] With FCC deregulation in the U.S., individual companies are permitted to dominate more markets since they are permitted to hold more media outlets within a given market area.

Theological and Ecclesial Responses to Globalization

Preachers have a unique opportunity to respond to injustices, particularly human rights violations, that result from globalization by telling the human stories of the victims, by identifying these "others" as brothers and sisters made in God's image. While Columbus wondered whether indigenous people had souls, Joerg Rieger insists that we *name* the "other" and affirm the person. He challenges us to do theology from the perspective of the "other," asking, "What if our blindness toward other people also produces a tragic blindness toward God, the Other?"[31]

In the 1960s, Gustavo Gutiérrez wrote that not only is God in the midst of the struggle for life, but also that God loves the poor and that they need to hear that God loves them.[32] Surrounded by an idolatrous market economy, can we reclaim a sacramental understanding of life, affirming in our preaching and teaching that God is with all of us and with all of creation? How can we restore balance on the planet through ethical means where the global market has caused imbalance?

Rev. Carmelo Alvarez, active in the Ecumenical Association of Third World Theologians (EATWOT),[33] recommends that we engage in these seven practices toward freeing those who are oppressed:[34]

1. Address the issues of globalization and local culture in light of the gospel.
2. Provide grounding in the spiritual traditions that would offset complacent acceptance of global injustices.
3. Continue seeking religious truth and discover how to practice love within the context of this seeking. Seeking truth is always dialogical; it involves a constant discernment and is part of the quest for human freedom.
4. Seek our identity as a pilgrim people throughout our journey. We have the capacity to adapt and to change as we become aware of our need for continual conversion.
5. Become aware of our interconnectedness with nature and all people, which counters the practice of isolating the poor.
6. As both relational and rational beings, refrain from actions that impact negatively on the poor.
7. Be people of moral integrity. Engage in the practice of forgiveness and believe that change can result from forgiveness and bring us closer to one another. Be reconcilers and recognize how

factors of our own lifestyles contribute to injustice. Believe that by acting out of our Christian faith we can help people become free.

Among the action steps recommended by the American Catholic Bishops in the 1991 document, "Renewing the Earth: An Invitation to Reflection and Action on Environment in Light of Catholic Social Teaching," was for "pastors and parish leaders to give greater attention to the extent and urgency of the environmental crisis in preaching, teaching, pastoral outreach, and action, at the parish level and through ecumenical cooperation in the local community."[35] How many preachers have addressed environmental and globalization concerns from the pulpit? In chapter 4 I discussed how preaching on disturbing news, such as climate change, may require the preacher to provide a great deal of background for listeners prior to preaching.

While theologians from developing countries write about the effects of globalization on their exploited poor, many advantaged westerners with superficial understanding may perceive globalization as an inconvenience, such as when dealing with call centers operated by workers in Asia or Africa, or perhaps interesting, when identifying the origin of purchases. Certainly the egregious ethical violations of manufacturing standards in certain exports from China have raised awareness that unsafe goods are becoming more common.[36] Preachers can help listeners gain a fuller perspective as they describe for their listeners the human rights challenges of globalization and the risks we face as consumers, along with the inclusive teachings of Jesus.

When Liberation Theology Turns Inward: The Challenge of Radical Islam, a Major Component of the News That Disturbs

Certainly at the center of much disturbing news in this century have been the activities of radical Islamists who claim they possess both religious and political authority as they seek to overturn the political and economic systems of the West.[37] Even before September 11, 2001, their acts of terrorism made disturbing news headlines.[38] The West's lack of knowledge about the tenets of Islam, as well as the origins and development of militant movements within radical Islam, put most preachers at a disadvantage in the weeks following the attacks on the Twin Towers in New York City and on the Pentagon, in Washington, D.C. It was too easy to draw simplistic conclusions about Islam from the acts of violent radicals who distort the precepts of their faith. Out of fear and ignorance, some prominent religious leaders made incorrect and intolerant pronouncements about the tenets of Islam and unfortunate remarks about solving the terrorist problem by entering into war with Iraq.[39]

Most of us haven't studied world religions, nor are we active in interfaith dialogue. While we encourage our listeners to study the Bible, Christian traditions, ethics and morality, we rarely discuss diversity within Christianity or the common values Christians share with members of other faith traditions. Unfortunately, our ignorance about the beliefs and practices of others can lead to prejudice. In this era of globalization and religious pluralism, those who proclaim that theirs as the only true religion diminish opportunities for building the trust and strong relationships between diverse people that are so needed in the world.[40]

Following 9/11, television media, especially PBS and CNN, aired instructive documentaries about radical or political Islam, while reminding viewers that Islam is practiced by millions of moderate, peaceful Muslims.[41] Might preachers prevent misunderstanding and mistrust with the Muslim "others" in our communities by inviting imams and leaders to meet and speak with congregation members? Our listeners need to receive accurate knowledge about Islam and its role in the lives of immigrants to the United States and American converts. *Newsweek*'s July 30, 2007, issue provided the inclusive coverage of Islam we need to increase understanding and reduce fear.[42]

During an interview celebrating the opening of a new mosque in Manassas, Virginia, Sheikh Rashid Lamptey, the new imam at Dar Al Noor, spoke about his response to 9/11 in terms of his faith:

> "I stood at Ground Zero, camera in hand," he recalled, his voice going deadly quiet with anger. "I tried to find a reason for people to do that. No reason appeared. I tried my very best. I couldn't find one simple reason that says we can throw a bomb or put an airplane into a building. I felt the melancholy, the weight of it, and I said, the time has come for us to stop using religion for ulterior motives, and teach people what religion stands for...It is up to us Muslims to put our religion out there and make it very transparent for people to see," he said, "and understand that this religion is not about bombing, it's not about killing, it's not about marrying 70 women in heaven, as I heard somebody say. It's about accountability; it's about sincerity; it's about forgiveness; it's about love."[43]

While today's expression of Islamic fundamentalism is rooted in a historical struggle for freedom from oppression, it differs from other liberation struggles in that radical Islamists use theology to *limit* freedom. Radical Islamists want to impose their ideology on all people. As Samir Amin expressed it, "Political Islam is the adversary of liberation theology. It advocates submission, not emancipation."[44]

Much of radical or political Islam is based on Wahhabi theology, a movement begun to purify Islam by eighteenth-century evangelist Muhammad ibn 'Abd al Wahab, who lived on the Arabian peninsula. Wahhabism espouses a literal interpretation of the Qu'ran, setting aside centuries of classical jurisprudential Islamic tradition, which had developed by the eleventh century to provide interpretations of the Qu'ran on all matters, including war, terrorism, and political violence.[45]

Building upon the proscriptions of the Prophet Muhammad, Muslim jurists insisted that there are legal restrictions upon the conduct of war. In general, Muslim armies may not kill women, children, seniors, hermits, pacifists, peasants, or slaves unless they are combatants. Vegetation and property may not be destroyed, water holes may not be poisoned, and flame-throwers may not be used unless out of necessity, and even then only to a limited extent. Torture, mutilation, and murder of hostages were forbidden under all circumstances. In contrast to their pragmatism regarding whether a war should be waged, the classical jurists accepted the necessity of moral constraints upon the way war is conducted.[46]

Wahhabism was used as a tool by the al Saud family to centralize their power as they conquered the Arabian peninsula in the 1920s. In its relations with the international community, the Saudi ruling family has tempered its association with this theology, but private money has helped fund a revised Wahhabism to flourish worldwide, including in some mosques in the United States.[47] Among its objectives is to remove the influence of the West from the Islamic world. Additionally, it seeks to purge Islam from movements, such as Sufism, which advocate a personal and mystical approach to Islam. Radical Islamists would implement *Sharia*, Muslim law based on the Qu'ran, in every area of life—civil, criminal and family. *Jihad* or holy war has become a visible result of this radicalization throughout the Muslim world, and has extended outward into Europe and Asia.[48] Moderate yet orthodox Muslim voices claim that this Islamic ideology proclaimed by Osama bin Laden and his followers is a perversion of Islam.

Islamic extremism took root in the Middle East during European colonial rule and gained influence during the post-colonial era.[49] The creation of Israel in 1948 radicalized Palestinians who grew more despondent as they were displaced from their homes and lost their livelihoods. Islamic fundamentalism and militancy gained momentum during the Iranian Islamic revolution in 1979 and the war in Afghanistan from 1979-1989. As disaffected men from several Arab states participated, Afghanistan became an important training ground for the globalization of Islamic terrorism.[50]

Terrorist attacks in Europe perpetrated by second and third generation Muslim immigrants in the years following 9/11 shocked the world. Waves of immigration beginning in 1945 brought Arabs seeking a better life, though most have not risen above a low living standard. A high percentage of their adult children are unemployed.[51] With little or no opportunity to be heard, even in European democratic societies, the mosque becomes the place where frustrated Muslim-European youth find support for jihad and reclaim their Muslim identity.[52]

The question of identity does not come up at all in traditional Muslim societies, as it did not in traditional Christian or Jewish societies. In a traditional Muslim society, an individual's identity is given by that person's parents and social environment; everything– from one's tribe and kin to the local imam to the political structure of the state–anchors one's identity in a particular branch of Islamic faith. It is not a matter of choice. Like Judaism, Islam is a highly legalistic religion, meaning that religious belief consists of conformity to a set of externally determined social rules. These rules are highly localized in accordance with the traditions, customs, saints, and practices of specific places. Traditional religiosity is not universalistic, despite Islam's doctrinal universalism.[53]

When Muslims emigrate to Western countries and no longer live in the midst of a traditional Muslim society, the vast differences between the two cultures can produce confusion and discomfort. Johns Hopkins University professor Francis Fukuyama suggests that while new immigrants bring their culture with them, second generation immigrant youth often disdain the culture and religion of their parents in spite of not assimilating into the new culture: "Stuck between two cultures with which they cannot identify, they find strong appeal in the universalist ideology of contemporary jihadism... Europe's failure to better integrate its Muslims is a ticking time bomb that has already contributed to terrorism."[54] In Fukuyama's view and that of Muslim leaders within the European Union, immigrants will need to develop pride in their new citizenship; and Europeans must make Muslim immigrants feel welcome. Muslims will also need to accept "liberal principles of individual equality" instead of trying "to challenge the secular character of the political order as a whole."[55]

What lessons can people in the United States learn from the experience of Europe's Muslim immigrants? How might preachers encourage their listeners to accept and assist immigrants as they adjust to their new community? Are there opportunities for the members of the congregation to meet socially with a Muslim community? How might pastors reach out to Muslim clergy in the area and establish a fruitful dialogue?

APPENDIX B

"Lament and Remember"
Message for May 25, 2008
2 Samuel 1-2:7

Introduction

1 and 2 Samuel are complicated books that deal with the period of time from the birth and call of Samuel, to the kingship of Saul, to the elevation of David as king. These were brutal times, when tribes were waging constant war. The good guys were the Israelites, while the other "ites" and the Philistines were enemies. Samuel was told by Yahweh to anoint Saul as king. The shepherd David came into the picture as a court musician. He enchanted listeners with his gifts as a composer and by playing the lyre and, as we know from the popular story, he became the fearless slayer of the giant Goliath.

Saul became jealous and fearful of David as David's popularity increased. Saul told his son Jonathan that he wanted to have David killed. However, by this time, Jonathan and David had become good friends and they even made an oath together in Yahweh's name. David left the north to engage in military operations in the south against the Amalekites, where he had his political base as a member of the tribe of Judah, though Saul continued to plot against him. (The Amalekites were a southern Palestinian nation hostile to Israel.) At this time the northern and southern tribes, constituting two kingdoms, were not yet united. David, himself, had the opportunity to kill Saul, but refrained from doing so. The duplicitous Saul even mustered an attempt at reconciliation, but it wasn't sincere.

At the end of 1 Samuel we find the first version of Saul's death at the hands of the Philistines on Mount Gilboa, which is in northern Israel. Saul realizes he is about to be killed and asks his armor bearer to kill him before the enemy gets to him. The armor-bearer froze, and Saul fell on his own sword. Saul, his three sons, including Jonathan, and all his men perished that day. The Israelites fled, and the

Philistines occupied the northern cities and displayed the decapitated heads, bodies and armor of Saul and his party.

At the rise of 2 Samuel, we read a different version of Saul's death. A young Amalekite immigrant tells of killing Saul and David fails to believe him, having him killed for being an opportunist trying to curry favor with him.

(2 Samuel 1–2:7 text is read here.)

Once upon a time, I was a Brownie and then a Girl Scout. Every Memorial Day we would march in a parade to the cemetery. There would be lots of flags and at some point Taps would be sounded. Then we'd all go home and enjoy the holiday, typically with a cookout. I'm not sure there was much lamenting or remembering, but the ceremonial parade with the playing of Taps surely honored the fallen service personnel from both world wars and the Korean conflict.

From my perspective now of age and experience, it seems to me that whatever we did was rather sanitized. I didn't get any message that war is hell. War was something that took place far away and seemed rather glorified. As I got older I became more fearful that we might be annihilated by the Russians. After all, we had all those air raid drills in school that heightened our fear and made us feel that Russians were our enemies. That all came back to me yesterday, when we enjoyed the new Indiana Jones film, *The Kingdom of the Crystal Skull.* It brought back the tensions of the 1950s with the nuclear arms race and the latent McCarthyism.

Then came the Vietnam War and young men of my age were trying very hard to get student deferments, knowing they had a good chance of being killed or wounded if they went over there. Eventually there was so much hostility to that war that, instead of taking it out on the government, our citizens took it out on the people who fought in it when they came home, although they had suffered greatly, many losing limbs and their mental functioning, many ending up on the streets, unemployed and unappreciated.

Now we are in the fifth year of another unpopular war. This weekend we are called to remember with gratitude those who served in the cause of freedom, especially those who lost their lives while serving. Remembering and thanking those who served is a good thing. Taking the time to honor the fallen is totally separate from our personal ideology of war. But that doesn't mean we can't vigorously oppose the ideology of waging war or that we shouldn't spend our lives trying to make peace in the name of the one who came to change the way we lived.

The passage from 2 Samuel is one of many in the Bible that illustrates the brutality of war and the conflicts that emerge when people choose to be divisive rather than uniting with one another for the common good. Even though Saul was so jealous that he felt compelled to destroy David, David comes off "bigger." He lamented Saul's death, and as well, of course, the death of his best friend Jonathan.

There is honesty in lament. It makes us stop and reflect. We may even change our course of action. Lament is rough. It can be angry. It may take shape as protest, complaint against God and against a situation. It may make us raise our voices against oppression and evil. The psalmists knew this and they expressed their true feelings as laments, including the one we just read in 2 Samuel that is attributed to David.

The constant warfare of the tribes in biblical times illustrated an ideology that war and killing were necessary to subdue people to grab their resources. Vengeance and retribution were normative. But Jesus insisted there was another way to behave. According to the gospels, violence was and is antithetical to his message of love that upholds the worth and dignity of everyone. So it is appropriate that we lament war and violence in any form and not be blindsided by those who tell us that war is inevitable.

We should remember the horrors of war and that should cause us to protest repeating war over and over. In the Iraq War, as of May 23, we lost more than 4,081 mostly young men and women, and we must remember them and pray for healing for their families. It is so hard to lose a child or a husband or a father or a mother. We must remember and pray for those many thousands returning with severe and limiting injuries, including PTSD (post-traumatic stress disorder), and an alarming rate of mental illness. A recent study reports these numbers: 300,000 vets have mental problems, 320,000 have had brain injuries.[1] We must lament the inadequate care that is being given our returning soldiers and pressure our representatives in Congress to act humanely to honor these people by caring for them properly.

Whenever we suffer loss, we look for new life to fill up the empty and hurting places. What positive things can come from our remembering and our lamenting this day? For me, I feel we must support those returning with disabilities and their families to gather the broken pieces of their lives into a process of wellness and wholeness. As Christians, it is appropriate for us must take responsibility for this and lament up and down until we get our way. We must remember the toll that war takes on individuals, not to mention a nation.

We must campaign for peace and not let leaders take us to places we don't need to go. If this sounds political, it's political in the sense that Jesus was political. He spoke out to get people to change how they treated other people. He demonstrated how all people are precious in God's sight. When we are able to conclude that every human life is precious, then we will decide that war is an absolute last resort, not something that Christians could normally consider a valid means for settling disputes.

We are the grass roots right here. It is up to us to see the face of Christ in every person and refrain from using physical or verbal violence. It's simply against what Jesus taught. The Good News is that the Old Testament tribal way of "tit for tat" was replaced by the gospel of Jesus. Suppose these words were on everyone's lips: "Blessed are the peacemakers, for they will be called children of God...Love your enemies and pray for those who persecute you." If putting into practice the vision of the non-violent Jesus isn't worth the effort, then he came and died in vain. I'm not prepared to give up on us.

On our prayer list we have several people connected to Pittsboro Christian who are serving in the military. Let us pray for their safety, honoring them today alongside those who have given their lives. Let us pray that their mission will become one of peacemaking, helping to secure and reconstruct the places that have endured destruction, leaving behind for the future a non-violent legacy to war in Iraq and Afghanistan. Let us pray for their safe return. Let us pray for our current and future leaders, that they will be people of peace. Let us pray for those whose experiences or the influence of others have distorted their sense of what is right, that their despair will lift and they will try peaceful means to solving their political and economic issues.

In this first decade of the twenty-first century after the birth of Jesus, there have been far too many occasions tempting us to lay aside the gospel of peace. Amid the brutality that perpetrators of violence exert all over the world, Christians will need to rally for solving problems peacefully, not retaliating with more violence. What do you see as your contribution to spreading the gospel of peace?

Will you join and support one of hundreds of peace organizations, including our own Disciples Peace Fellowship? Will you pray daily for peace? Will you support peace initiatives that come to you on the Internet, such as the work of Amnesty International or Human Rights Watch? Perhaps you will feel called to take part in demonstrations. Please take this question home to ponder: How will you allow the gospel of peace to penetrate you and influence others as a peacemaker in the name of Jesus?

APPENDIX C

"If the Roof Is an Obstacle…"
Sermon for February 16, 2003
Psalm 41, Mark 2:1-12

They couldn't possibly pass up the opportunity. Who knew how long Jesus would be staying in Capernaum? The attention of the crowd was on his preaching–all they needed to do was figure out a way to get their friend inside. Ingenious–can't get through the crowd? Climb up and cut a hole into the roof. How's that for the determination of a group of people to find healing for a paralyzed friend. How did they even know that Jesus would be able to heal him? That's simple. They believed the testimony of others who attested to Jesus' gift. They had faith he could do it again. Wouldn't you go the distance to find healing for someone you love? Even if the treatment was experimental? And surely attempting to be healed by this Jesus was brand new treatment!

Because of what he said in curing the paralyzed man, Jesus revealed to all present that he had the authority to heal and forgive sins. The scribes accuse him of blasphemy. "Only God can forgive sins." Jesus was endangering his own life, laying the groundwork for his own death. You just don't go around telling everyone that you have authority to do what only God can do. But that didn't stop the people from praising God for what they had seen.

The psalmist who gave us Psalm 41 begins with praise for deliverance:

"Happy are those who consider the poor; the Lord delivers them in the day of trouble. The Lord protects them and keeps them alive. As for me, I said, 'O Lord, be gracious to me; heal me, for I have sinned against you.'"

Our world is in great need of healing. Do you agree? At no other time in my adult life can I reflect with greater sadness on a world that fallen into such great sin. Oh, you and I are no more sinful than we've always been. We have our little problems with people. We may be less generous and tolerant than we should be. Maybe we say things we regret. No, for the most part we uphold the rights of others, we worship and praise our God regularly. We vote, pay taxes, support the church. We're not the problem—or are we?

Yesterday, millions of people, all over the world held rallies against going to war in Iraq. Millions of people. Though I was ready with a professional-looking sign in my car, I didn't take part downtown because of the weather. While I'm disappointed in my lack of follow-through, I was so proud of those people who said no to war, who concluded that no one has presented evidence to justify starting violence that would result in the death of five hundred thousand people. People are beginning to say with some conviction that war is our failure to deal with reconciliation.

Roderick Hart wrote *The Political Pulpit*, published by Purdue University Press, in 1977. Its premise was that there is a social contract that keeps the civil and religious institutions from meddling in each other's affairs. That presupposed that the churches wouldn't speak out on public policy. After 9/11, there was a panel organized to review Hart's thoughts and *The Journal of Communication and Religion* came out with an entire issue in March 2002 that discusses the connection between politics and religion in America, a kind of retrospective that includes a last chapter by Hart himself.

As a minister, I am very troubled that my colleagues and I might keep from expressing our thoughts about political matters because we might be trying to protect the viability of church institutions. Surely the experience of the German church during the Third Reich should have been all we need to know that silence is paralysis. Silence may as well be an affirmation.

I believe that preachers along with the rest of the people of God must look to the teachings of Jesus in times like this. The over-used, but nonetheless apt question: What would Jesus do? is our question. For me, I admit that I am trying to be a follower of the non-violent Jesus, the one who spent his ministry healing and preaching the character of the kingdom of God.

That was the difference between the faith of the paralytic and the faith of the psalmist. The psalmist laments: "Even my bosom friend in whom I trusted, who ate of my bread, has lifted the heel against me. But you, O Lord, be gracious to me and raise me up, that I may repay them. By this I know that you are pleased with me; because my enemy has not triumphed over me."

The paralytic's life is forever changed. He takes up his mat, and like the leper and the tax collectors and the man with a withered hand, all of these early chapters of Mark's gospel, the good news is that they move on. They don't stay stuck or paralyzed in old ways of thinking. Their healing changes them. The psalmist is looking for retribution. Jesus taught us to love even our enemies.

I received two articles on Friday. One from the February 11 edition of the *Christian Science Monitor* called "War, Peace Collide in Sermons: Many Churches Oppose Iraq Action and Ministers Say So," by Kim Campbell. The other is called "Patriotism is Not Enough: Christian conscience in time of war," by Peter Gomes in *Sojourners Magazine*. Rev. Gomes serves Harvard Memorial Church and teaches moral theology at Harvard Divinity School. The article was adapted from a sermon he gave last October.

Gomes raised the question: "What do you do when your country is headed where you think your faith and your God don't want you to go?" According to the article from the *Christian Science Monitor*, preachers from many churches, synagogues, and mosques are speaking of peace in sermons and in public, while others are saying nothing. One frustrated woman from Pennsylvania said she hears nothing from the pulpit about war or antiwar sentiment and she thinks the preachers are concerned about the collection dropping if they bring it up. Locally, a peace-activist friend was prevented from distributing a notice about yesterday's peace rally in last Sunday's bulletin. The reason? His pastor told him it would anger the Republicans.

The Word of God must not be trapped or held hostage by politics. Christ's Spirit must not be imprisoned anywhere, least of all in the sanctuaries where we turn for nurture and direction, where we come to collectively seek out God's will for us, where we join together in affirming our faith in him who died for our sins so that we would not continue to inflict pain on one another.

Above all, we must not be silent. If we feel convicted that war is justified, we need to share our reasons and set them in context with the Christian scripture. Likewise, if war is absolutely the last resort for our consciences, we need to be prepared for the consequences of not striking first. Peace has its price. War has its price. But silent paralysis will not achieve peace and will not convince anyone to go to war.

Again, from the Gomes sermon: "I know that in the mighty roar of wisdom, might, and riches, the sounds of love, justice, and righteousness—those things in which God delights, and in which God's people are meant to delight—sound thin, feeble, and anemic. Yet my Christian conscience tells me that these "soft" values should prevail every time over the "hard," even though they often do not. If I am compelled to compromise those Christian values in the service of the state, I had better be as certain as is humanly possible that such a compromise is worth sacrificing the things I hold most precious; and I certainly won't know that, nor will you, unless there is a great deal more thoughtful discussion, debate, and dissent than there has been so far."

The National Council of Churches, leaders of individual denominations, including the Disciples, as well as the United States Conference of Catholic Bishops, have spoken out; groups have taken out billboard and television ads. Religious people united together should be powerful. We can all share our positions with the president and our members of Congress.

An Ohio pastor lost a couple of families from his 530-household church due to the church's anti-war position, though others who disagreed have stayed. This pastor said for the *Monitor:* "Our fundamental calling as people of faith is to be makers of peace, and that's a very public calling. If we don't speak out in times like these, then we concede the field to those who are willing to speak."

Blessed be your response in the days ahead. Pray for peace and for the peacemakers. May the teaching of Jesus, Healer, the Prince of Peace, guide our prayer and our actions.

Survey about News

(1=regularly, 2=sometimes, 3=rarely or never)

1. How do you become aware of news events?
   ____ newspaper
   ____ television
   ____ Internet
   ____ radio
   ____ conversation

2. How frequently do you consult news sources?
   ____ once a day
   ____ several times a day
   ____ (how many?) times a day

3. Have you ever been disturbed, shocked, or frightened by a news story? (For purposes of this questionnaire, "to disturb" means "to create anxiety.")
   ____ yes ____ no

4. Which level of news event is likely to disturb you?
   ____ local news
   ____ national news
   ____ international news

5. Of the following, which are likely to disturb you when they appear as prominent news events?
   ____ street violence
   ____ domestic violence
   ____ war
   ____ terrorism in the U.S.

_____ terrorism abroad
_____ unstable financial markets
_____ corporate fraud
_____ sexual misconduct
_____ illegal drugs
_____ forest fires
_____ earthquakes and hurricanes
_____ issues in proximity to family members, i.e. natural
     disasters, political upheaval
_____ disease epidemics
_____ environmental problems, i.e. oil spills
_____ labor strife
_____ injustice toward individuals
_____ poverty
_____ welfare system
_____ health care
_____ globalization issues involving injustice toward
     populations
_____ celebrity scandals
_____ elections
_____ political decisions
_____ additional, please list:

6. Can you name critical issues that have made the news that
are rooted in human struggle, especially in the struggle for
freedom? Can you briefly describe the struggle, as well as the
underlying causes of the struggle?

7. Do you feel that preachers should deal with disturbing news
events from the pulpit?
    _____ yes _____ no
comment:

8. Have you ever attended a worship service during a time
of crisis and left disappointed that the preacher had not
incorporated the news that disturbed you into the preaching?

_____ yes _____ no
comment:

9. Can you describe an experience when you heard a sermon
delivered by a preacher who responded to a crisis or to a
disturbing news event?

10. In your opinion, is preaching about the news that disturbs
desirable as part of pastoral care for a congregation?

_____ yes _____ no
comment:

11. What suggestions do you have for preachers as they prepare to
preach to a community that may be disturbed by particular
news events?

12. In which areas of knowledge should your preacher be well
    informed?

  ____ local issues

  ____ national issues

  ____ international issues

  ____ liberation theologies (struggles against injustice in
    the light of faith)

  ____ economic trends

  ____ politics

  ____ popular culture

  ____ ecology and environmental issues

  ____ basic psychology theory

  ____ family dynamics

  ____ world religions

  ____ other, please list:

13. In your opinion, should a preacher be a "mediator of the news
    and the Good News?" That is, do you expect or want your
    preacher to deal with the critical issues facing us that may be
    disturbing?

  ____ yes ____ no

  comment:

APPENDIX E

"Stocking the Spiritual Pantry"

Message for June 1, 2008

Genesis 6:9–9:17

Today's lesson, the story of Noah and the Flood, is especially relevant in light of the major disasters that occurred in Asia last month. A few weeks ago we were all saddened by the loss of life and desperate circumstances that the people of Myanmar faced as Cyclone Nargis hit their country. We are appalled as their government fails to provide for its estimated 2.4 million homeless and hungry citizens. At least 134,000 are dead or missing. (Associated Press report in The Indianapolis Star, A4, May 31, 2008.)

Even while we were trying to comprehend the severity of the cyclone, the people of China experienced a devastating earthquake, with a death toll now of nearly 70,000 with 5 million people homeless, and tragic news continues to pour in as the people cope with this natural disaster of monumental proportions. Here in America, tornados have been taking their toll on the people of several Midwestern and Western states, with several deaths impacting local communities. Even here, tornados this past Friday night caused widespread damage, with millions of dollars of damage to property and several hundred people homeless.

How do we respond to the tragedies of our brothers and sisters? What can we do and what do we do? We know we can easily contribute to relief efforts by going online or sending in money to Week of Compassion, our denomination's agency that works with relief groups all over the world. We know we can pray for the people who experience directly the loss of homes and loved ones. We can reach out to families and friends of those affected, such as the Disciples congregation in Indianapolis that is made up largely of refugees from Myanmar or Burma. We can inquire of those in our midst at work or elsewhere who may have families in the devastated areas.

We can even try to hook up with church or other groups that rebuild communities after disasters, as several of our congregations have been doing as a response to Hurricane Katrina. Or, we may be among those with construction and carpentry skills who can volunteer in Indianapolis.

But I suggest there's something else we can do when we are mourning the losses of others. We can prepare *ourselves* spiritually to be ready to respond *faithfully* should tragedies or disasters impact us. What I mean by that is that we plan to increase the reserves in our spiritual pantry that help us as we experience a range of life's challenges. Like jars of garden produce some of us prepare for consumption throughout the winter, we can "put up" a stockpile of stories and experiences that reaffirm God's love and presence even when dire circumstances may make us feel God and God's care for us is absent.

"But," you say, "don't we just jump in and get to work when something happens?" Well, some of us do and others crumble when faced with a crisis that requires faith. Some of us grow weary fighting challenges in our lives and there can be that "one more thing" capable of driving us over the edge to despair.

The stories of the Bible that we hear in worship, that many of us have grown up with, and that we study in groups or individually, provide a treasure trove for shaping our faith and for laying a foundation for coping in bad times, as well as good times. They are one hedge against depression.

Even in these early stories from Genesis that are based on myths in wide circulation, (and there were at least twenty-five flood stories in ancient literature), we can deal with the themes of judgment, understand them in term of their time and setting, and extract from them the major themes of hope and new life.

In a very loose sense, the stories from the Book of Genesis give us a biography of our early ancestors of faith. They were ornery like we are sometimes. They sinned, sometimes with terrible repercussions, and they often lost their way. They were violent and destructive. According to the narrative, God selected one righteous old man, his wife and his descendents, with two representatives from each barnyard species and the general animal kingdom, as a remnant to start over, hopefully with a better result.

Although it may be difficult for some of us to get past the idea that God would destroy the Creation that God loved into existence, what I get out of this story is that goodness will prevail somehow, even when it is confronted by incomprehensible adversity. The writer does describe the Great Flood as God's premeditated work to eradicate the people who had made a mess of creation. In fact, God expresses regret for creating humankind. The human storyteller attributed human emotion to God. In our humanness, it's easy for us to blame God for disasters and all of our misfortunes.

Insurance companies perpetuate blaming disasters on God by calling cyclones, earthquakes, tornados, or floods "acts of God." However, as people of faith, and in keeping with who we are as Disciples, we will be careful about theologizing about natural disasters or even pandemic health crises as being God's will. In fact, in light of our Christian faith, their occurrences should evoke great compassion, not smug judgment.

The end game for God in the Flood story consists of these two points that are essential for us and our faith: God will deliver the people and God is committed to life. Out of chaos order comes eventually and with it new life, if we have the patience to remain spiritually alive in the present. The problem for us westerners in the twenty-first century is that with our linear thinking we expect things to be taken care of swiftly and when they aren't we can lose hope.

But we need to be reminded that we live in the present, where no future exists as yet. That doesn't mean we can't envision a future of new life. We just don't know until we're in it, what that new life will be. At a recent funeral, I commented that the deceased left a legacy for the future of some thirty descendents and that, although they were naturally sad that their loved one left this world, she had provided for decades of ever-evolving new life in that family, if they carry her memory with them, acting faithfully and lovingly as she did.

Even without mammoth-scale disasters, we know we are vulnerable to so many personal issues that can upend us, such as economic problems, health issues, lack of mobility and the loss of those close to us. The stories of the Bible comfort us in some ways because they let us know that our fears and our responses to events are normal.

The way we not only survive but thrive in adversity is by acting with a lively faith and for many of us that faith is practiced in community. God's love is channeled through us when we reach out to someone hurting. A community of faith can remind everyone within it and outside it that they are beloved of God, especially in the moments when some people may feel bereft and forlorn. The grace to strengthen another's resolve is of God and through our faith we receive that grace. Do you remember how that played out in the book of Ruth with Ruth and Naomi as Ruth stood by her mother-in-law?

Then there are the stories about Jesus healing, often simply with his presence and attentiveness. When we read and re-read those stories, we absorb the message that the love of God in Christ is as persistent as the woman's search for the lost coin, or shepherd's for the lost sheep.

It's valuable to have resources to keep ourselves and others from climbing into the "pit." When bad things happen, we may instead need to climb aboard the *ark* and start over, making decisions grounded faith about how we will live.

I am still moved by the faith of a pastor in Alabama, who gathered enormous resources of grace and courage when a tornado tore through her church, killing twenty people, including her daughter. It was the week before Easter. I can't imagine how difficult it was for her to deal with her grief and that of her congregation and still preach on Easter Sunday. Nonetheless, she was able to minister to her congregation by asking two questions that came out of her personal tragedy and out of her faith: "What am I going to do with the life I have today, with the family members I have today, with the church I have today? How can we be the comforting church when we're all suffering?"

Think of the stories that help us grow into mature faith as jars lined up on the shelves of our spiritual pantry. Consider how these narratives can help us make connections with what we go through, stories—because we can remember stories easier than abstract ideas. That's why the narratives surrounding the story of the Exodus have encouraged oppressed people that freedom will come. That's why relating the passion story of Jesus helps us understand pain, rejection, sacrifice for others, as well as the hope of eternal life. That's why a tale about Sarah or Elizabeth conceiving a child when they thought that period of their lives was over inspires hope to never say never.

When our faith and resolve, our energy and commitment may waver, we can open up these jars containing all the stories of our faith, finding inspiration in those that will lead us to new life. What stories and scripture verses will you place in your faith jars for preserving in your spiritual pantry?

I'd like to extend this conversation over the summer and include some of your responses in the next three newsletters. It might make a difference to some of us if we purposely stock the spiritual pantry so we can always reach in to support our faith and the faith of others, even during difficult times.

APPENDIX F

"National Day of Prayer and Remembrance"

Homily for September 14, 2001

Ephesians 6:10–17 and Matthew 28:16–20

I don't know where it came from, but sitting on top of my computer at home is a framed card that says: "In our weakest times God's strength is ours to trust. In our saddest times, His compassion is ours to heal. In all times His love is ours to share."

My brothers and sisters, this awful tragedy that continues to stir our feelings into anger, grief, disbelief, and perhaps fear, will not overcome us—as people who know that Good will triumph over Evil, as Jesus triumphed over the Cross.

The power of Evil is palpable. We can feel it even as new leads are uncovered that tell us this was as premeditated an operation as could be. The idea was to kill our spirit, to bring us down, to cause us even to abandon our hope, our trust, our love for the God of life. This attack is about the power of Evil over Good. Evil is a misuse of our God-given freedom. It is the wrong choice. The energy that went into planning and executing this horror was the energy of pure evil.

In 1941, sixty years ago on a Sunday morning, men, women, and children awakened to the news of the destruction of the naval fleet in Pearl Harbor, and with it the deaths of many people who loved and were loved.

This week all men, women, and children of our country spent Tuesday losing our innocence as we faced the reality that no matter how we plan, no matter how we see ourselves or others see us in control, we cannot control some of the world's evil, and that is humbling. You may remember that a couple of Sundays ago I quoted Joan Chittister as saying "Humility is reality to the full." It doesn't get any fuller and we have been humbled.

But dear children, think about how you feel when you fall down and scrape your knees. It hurts and putting medicine on it to make it better sometimes hurts, too. But then in a few days, it hurts less and the knee heals. And, after the worst things happen to us, we do heal, we go on living, go on loving, hopefully learning new lessons about living and loving better. But going back to hurting our knee, we may not forget that we fell down because maybe we'll have a scar on our knee and even when we're older, we may point to that scar (and I speak from experience) and tell the story of how we got it.

Likewise, we won't ever forget what took place on Tuesday. It will remain as a scar deep within our American heart. But how we can turn that scar into remembrance is to grow and learn how to be disciples of peace, to go and serve the Lord by preaching all that Jesus commanded, especially the commandment to love our neighbor. We must see ourselves as a tiny, but vital contribution to life, becoming a gift to all who know us, treating each other as though each of us is Christ, making sure that quarrels are patched up, that good things are said, that bad stuff never grows into a force of energy that is converted to Evil.

Dear children, please don't fear for the dead. They are safe with the Lord. Please pray for the children who have lost their parents, and learn to value your parents even more as a result of this tragedy. Don't live in fear at all, but in the hope and trust that our faith teaches us.

Be angry and grieve, but take time to be quiet each day and let your emotions surface that you are controlling, especially if you are a professional who is covering your feelings on the job. Take time to pray and be present within the Mystery of God, the Mystery of life that defies understanding or control.

Understand that everyone is affected by the tremendous stress of this time and that tempers are short and people are irritable. Be extra patient with everyone. In fact, combat the ferocity of this unholy evil with Christian discipleship. Be love and peace and know the truth. Share the Good News: "Teach them to observe all that I have commanded you. And behold, I am with you always…"

Notes

Introduction

[1]In *Time* magazine, May 31, 1963, "(Barth) recalls that 40 years ago he advised young theologians 'to take your Bible and take your newspaper, and read both. But interpret newspapers from your Bible...' Newspapers, he says, are so important that I always pray for the sick, the poor, journalists, authorities of the state and the church – in that order. Journalists form public opinion. They hold terribly important positions. Nevertheless, a theologian should never be formed by the world around him – either East or West. He should make his vocation to show both East and West that they can live without a clash. Where the peace of God is proclaimed, peace on earth is implicit. Have we forgotten the Christmas message?"

[2]See the Center for Media Literacy's Web site and Media Awareness Network's Web site http://www.media-awareness.ca/english/issues/index.cfm.

[3]The Pew Research Center for the People and the Press/The Pew Forum on Religion and Public Life, *Survey: Different Faiths, Different Messages: Americans Hearing About Iraq From the Pulpit, But Religious Faith Not Defining Opinions.* Washington, DC: March 19, 2003, available at http://pewforum.org/surveys/.

Chapter 1: Preaching and the News That Disturbs

[1]Luke 4:18–19

[2]Audrey Borschel. "Find the Common Ground," in *Theology of Preaching: Essays on Vision and Mission in the Pulpit,* ed. Gregory Heille, O.P. (London: Melisende, 2001), 73–74.

[3]William J. Nottingham, *The Practice and Preaching of Liberation* (St. Louis: CBP Press, 1986), 26.

[4]Javier Navia, *La Nación,* Buenos Aires (Dec. 30, 2001), reprinted in *World Press Review* 49, no. 3 (March 2002), http://www.worldpress.org/0302top10.htm.

[5]These two Web sites provide detailed information about the European countries' response to terrorism: http://www.diplomatic.be/EN/policy/policynotedetail. asp?TEXTID=13623 and http://news.bbc.co.uk/2/hi/europe/7355446.stm.

[6]RAND Center for Military Health Policy Research, April 18, 2008, http://rand. org/pubs/monographs/2008/RAND_MG720.pdf.

[7]George Will, "Last surviving doughboy links past to present," *The Indianapolis Star,* May 26, 2008, A14.

[8]Information from www.guardian.co.uk/world/zimbabwe, March 24, 2008.

[9]Information from http://www.foxnews.com/story/0,2933,258926,00.html.

[10]From http://www.politicallore.com/economy/federal-reserve-chairman-ben-bernanke-predicts-recession/206, April 2, 2008.

[11]In an Associated Press article released on January 2, 2008, both ABC and FOX announced they would exclude less prominent candidates from debates. *The New York Times'* David Brooks commented on the January 3, 2008, PBS *Newshour* that a candidate's celebrity status affects the amount of media coverage, thus the better-known candidate receives more media attention.

[12]From www.firstamendment.org.

[13]James Madison, *Federalist Papers,* No. 51, available at http://friesian.com/ quotes.htm. "But what is government itself but the greatest of all reflections on human nature? If men were angels, no government would be necessary. If angels were to govern men, neither external nor internal controls on government would be necessary. In framing a government which is to be administered by men over men, the great difficulty lies in this: You must first enable the government to control the governed; and in the next place, oblige it to control itself. A dependence on the

167

people is no doubt the primary control on the government; but experience has taught mankind the necessity of auxiliary precautions."

[14]From www.merriamwebster.com/dictionary/politics.

[15]William Loader, "Will you at this time restore the kingdom to Israel?" (Acts 1:6), http://wwwstaff.murdoch.edu.au/~loader/BeingtheChurch1.htm.

[16]Richard A. Horsley, *Jesus and Empire* (Minneapolis: Fortress Press, 2003), 86.

[17]Loader, "Will you at this time restore the kingdom to Israel?"

[18]The Rev. Jacob Duche offered prayer at the start of the Continental Congress on September 7, 1774. See http://www.christianlaw.org/articles/public_prayer2. html.

[19]Methodist minister and justice activist James Wolfe offered this definition during a lecture for the Global Peace and Justice Day at Marian University, April 30, 2008.

[20]Robert Bellah, "Civil Religion in America," *Daidalus,* Journal of the American Academy of Arts and Sciences, Religion in America, 96, no. 1 (Winter 1967): 1–21.

[21]Roderick P. Hart, *The Political Pulpit* (West Lafayette, Ind.: Purdue Univ. Press, 1977).

[22]*The Journal of Communication and Religion* 25, no. 1 (March 2002).

[23]For an excellent description of religious language in President Bush's speeches, see "The Danger for America Is Not Theocracy," speech delivered by Michael Gerson, speechwriter and policy advisor to President Bush, December 2004, The Ethics and Public Policy Center, published at www.beliefnet.com/story/159/story_15943_1. html.

[24]Ruben Navarette, from "There's no holy war in the heartland," *The Indianapolis Star,* December 20, 2007. Conflict helps sell magazines, but *Newsweek* went overboard in framing the Huckabee-Romney contest as an exercise in religious strife. There are at least three problems with this narrative–it's dangerous, insulting, and likely untrue. Dangerous because it provides yet another way to divide Americans. Insulting because it paints a large swath of the Iowa electorate as religious bigots. And likely untrue because *Newsweek's* own polling data suggest that Iowans are more open-minded than national political commentators give them credit for being.

[25]Mark Jurkowitz, "The Pastor's Press Tour Is the Week's Big Newsmaker," Project for Excellence in Journalism, May 8, 2008, http://freepress.net/node/39548/print.

[26]"Religion and Culture: Meeting the Challenge of Pluralism." Transcript of audio press conference, February 11, 2003. See http://www.religionandpluralism.org/ANC_transcript_President_or_Preacher.htm.

[27]Ibid.

[28]"An Evangelical Manifesto: A Declaration of Evangelical Identity and Public Commitment," Washington, D.C., May 7, 2008:15, available online at www.anevangelicalmanifesto.com.

[29]Editorial, *The Christian Century* (March 8, 2003): 5. An article on 10–11 discusses Bush's religious rhetoric as reported in various print and electronic news sources. Also in the same issue Robert Bellah contributed "Righteous Empire," which explores the themes surrounding an American imperialism.

[30]Much has been written about the response of conservative Christians to the Iraq War. These articles provide information from 2002–2003, and from 2007: Jim Lobe, "Conservative Christians Biggest Backers of Iraq War," Oct. 10, 2002 entry, http://commondreams.org/headlines02/1010-02.htm; Don Monkerud, "The Great Christian Schism," www.counterpunch.org/monkerud05092003.html; Robert Marus, "Christians & the War", and "Do conservative evangelicals regret justifying Iraq War?," ABP Washington Bureau, *The Baptist Standard,* 1.19.07, www.baptiststandard. com; "Democracy slams 'Leftist' National Council of Churches," January 19, 2007, www.mediatransparency.org.

[31]Martin J. Medhurst, "Forging a Civil-Religious Construct for the 21st Century," *The Journal of Communication and Religion* 25 (March 2002): 91.

[32]Pierre Atlas, "We can take stand on Darfur," *The Indianapolis Star*, April 12, 2007, A12.

[33]Tony Campolo, "What Is Liberation Theology?" http://newsweek. washingtonpost.com/onfaith/guestvoices/2008/04/what_is_liberation_theology. html.

[34]Joerg Rieger. *God and the Excluded: Visions and Blindspots in Contemporary Theology* (Minneapolis: Fortress Press, 2001). A careful reading of Rieger's methodology provides a general blueprint for understanding, in a theological context, the commonalities of oppression.

[35]These sniper attacks were taking place in October 2002, in the beltway area of Washington, D.C. at the time the questionnaire was completed. Ten people were killed and three were seriously injured.

Chapter 2: The News as Commerce

[1]Walter Cronkite, from keynote address, February 6, 2007, Columbia Graduate School Forum on Media Ownership.

[2]*The Times* said up to seventy jobs could be cut from its news operations, which would reduce the newsroom staff to about 850 people. *The Times* news operation employed about 1,200 when it was bought by Tribune in 2000. *The Times'* Jeffrey Johnson resigned in 2006 after protesting Tribune's proposed cuts. See http:// abclocal.go.com/kgo/story?section=nation_world&id=4632184.

[3]David Folkenflik, National Public Radio, "Recording Shows Tribune Owner Zell's Fiery Side," April 8, 2008, at http://freepress.net/node/38311/print.

[4]Jean Yves Chainon, *The Editors Weblog*, March 6, 2008, "The press release and cost cut problem: editorial forgetting and core values? www.editorsweblog. org/2008/03/.

[5]Ibid.

[6]Greg Mitchell, "UPDATE: Clinton-Obama Debate: ABC Slammed for Focus on 'Trivial Issues,'" April 19, 2008, http://www.editorandpublisher.com/eandp/news/ article_display.jsp?vnu_content_id=1003790556.

[7]*Bill Moyers Journal*, April 25, 2007, transcript at http://www.pbs.org/moyers/ journal/btw/transcript1.html.

[8]University of Oregon School of Journalism and Communication, "RTNDA Code of Broadcast News Ethics," 2002, http://jcomm.uoregon.edu/about/ethics/ rtnda.html, [November 15, 2002].

[9]Lee Thayer, Hanno Hardt, and Richard L. Johannesen, eds., *Ethics, Morality and the Media* (New York: Hastings House, 1980), 97.

[10]*Bill Moyers Journal*, April 25, 2007.

[11]From http://library.wustl.edu/units/spec/filmandmedia/collections/hampton/ eyes1/ashmore.htm. Quoting from the Web site: "Ashmore's contribution to the Civil Rights Movement is best summarized in his reporting on the Little Rock School Crisis of 1957. Ashmore and *The Arkansas Gazette* each received a Pulitzer Prize for the advancement of defiant views on integration. This was a huge, and unprecedented moment in American history. He openly espoused integration, leading the way for writers and civilians alike to start thinking differently about the state of justice in the United States."

[12]Ibid.

[13]Thayer et al., *Ethics, Morality*, 81.

[14]Cenk Uygur, "The media isn't supposed to be neutral," *The Huffington Post*, May 7, 2006, http://www.huffingtonpost.com/cenk-uygur/the-media-isnt-supposed- _b_20521.html

[15]For a comprehensive list of links to foreign newspapers see www. Watchingamerica.com/index.shtml#newssources.

[16]Jim Crane, "Al-Jazeera big in English, not in U.S.," http://www.boston.com/ news/world/middleeast/articles/2007/04/17/al_jazeera_bib_in_eng... April 17, 2007.

[17]Roger Cohen, "Bring the Real World Home," http://www.nytimes.com/2007/11/12/opinion/12cohen.html?n=Top/News/World/Columns/Roger%20Cohen.

[18]Margrit Cromwell, USA, comment on blog site of *International Herald Tribune*, http://blogs.iht.com/tribtalk/opinion/passages/?p=44.

[19]Sue Halligan, St. Paul, Minn., ibid.,

[20]Brent Cunningham, "Dave Marash: Why I Quit," *Columbia Journalism Review* (April 4, 2008), http://www.cjr.org/the_water_cooler/dave_marash_why_i_quit.php?page=all.

[21]Eric Pfanner, "Al Jazeera English Tries to Extend Its Reach," May 19, 2008, http://www.nytimes.com/2008/05/19/business/media/19jazeera.html?th=&emc=th&pagew.

[22]Ben Bagdikian. "The Lord of the Global Village," *The Nation* (June 12, 1989), 119.

[23]Bruce B. Brugmann, April 20, 2007, commenting on the history of media monopolies in light of current newspaper buyouts in the San Francisco Bay area and his relationship with Bagdikian during the years between editions of Bagdikian's book, www.sfbg.com/blogs/bruce/2007/04/a_guest_blog_item_by_ben_bagdi.html.

[24]Ben Bagdikian, *The New Media Monopoly* (Boston: Beacon Press, 2004), 3.

[25]Ibid., 14 and 25.

[26]Richard Siklos, "In Murdoch's Past, Clues to the Journal's Future," http://www.nytimes.com/2007/08/01/business/media/01murdoch.html?pagewanted=2&th&emc=th.

[27]James Fallows, "The Age of Murdoch," *TheAtlantic.com,* September 2003, http://www.theatlantic.com/doc/200309/fallows.

[28]Ibid.

[29]Bagdikian, *The New Media Monopoly,* 207.

[30]The Web site www.cjr.org/tools/owners from Columbia School of Journalism provides details of corporate ownership.

[31]*Bill Moyers Journal,* October 25, 2002, transcript available at http://www.pbs.org/now/transcript/transcript_bmjfcc.html.

[32]"New Federal Rules for Media Ownership: How Much Does the Public Know?" Project for Excellence in Journalism, 2003, www.journalism.org. The survey was taken between February 12 and 18, 2003, with the Pew Research Center for the People and Press and the Project for Excellence in Journalism.

[33]Brian Lambert. "Networks were silent on FCC story," *Pioneer Press* (June 5, 2003). See http://www/twincities.com/mld/pioneerpress/entertainment/6015141.htm.

[34]In his op-ed piece in *The New York Times* on June 29, 2007, Paul Krugman described the process used by Rupert Murdoch to slant the news to "serve his business interests." Murdoch, whose company News Corporation owns Fox News, had been negotiating to buy controlling interest in *The Wall Street Journal.* The concern, according to Krugman, is that Murdoch micromanages his news organizations through exaggeration, misleading the public, as in the Fox News hyping the weapons of mass destruction in Iraq, or by failing to report stories that don't fit his political agenda. See http://query.nytimes.com/search/query?frow=0&n=10&srcht=a&query=&srchst=nyt&hdlquery=&bylquery=Paul+Krugman&daterange=period&mon1=06&day1=29&year1=2007&mon2=06&day2=30&year2=2007&submit.x=18&submit.y=7.

[35]The Senate Commerce Committee passed the bipartisan "Media Ownership Act of 2007," hoping to address the dwindling number of media outlets owned by women and minorities, as well as the cross-ownership of media in one city. See "Senate OKs Media Bill," Associated Press story, Dec. 5, 2007, www.freepress.net/news/28758.

[36]John Eggerton, "FCC Loosens Newspaper-Broadcast Cross-Ownership Limits," *Broadcasting & Cable,* 12/18/07, http://www.broadcastingcable.com/article/CA6513656.html

[37]Robert W. McChesney and Hohn Nichols, "Who'll Unplug Big Media? Stay Tuned," *The Nation* (May 29, 2008), http://www.freepress.net/node/41013.

[38]H.R. 5994: To amend the Clayton Act with respect to competitive and nondiscriminatory access to the Internet. The legislation was introduced by Rep. John Conyers of Michigan May 8, 2008.

[39]See www.freepress.com for current news about legislation and action steps for citizens.

[40]For excellent background article see http://www.museum.tv/archives/etv/A/htmlA/army-mccarthy/army-mccarthy.htm.

[41]Walter Davis et al., eds. *Watching What We Watch: Prime-Time Television through the Lens of Faith,* (Louisville: Geneva Press, 2001), 210. This book provides a historical overview of television news and current events coverage that places the growth and influence of television in perspective.

[42]Charles Colson, "Colson: Victory over Napalm," *Christianity Today* 41, no. 3 (March 3, 1997): 96. See http://www.christianitytoday.com/ct/713096.html. Also see http://www.washingtonpost.com/wp-srv/onpolitics/watergate/charles.html. President Nixon's Special Counsel Charles W. Colson served seven months in prison in 1974 after pleading guilty to obstruction of justice in the Watergate-related Daniel Ellsberg case. He became a born-again Christian and in 1976 founded the Prison Fellowship Ministries.

[43]Davis et al., *Watching,* 224.

[44]CBS's newsmagazine *60 Minutes,* June 20, 2003, available at http://archives.museum.tv/.

[45]Elizabeth Jensen, "Lehrer Says 'News Hour' Money Woes are Worst Ever," *The New York Times,* May 19, 2008, http://www.nytimes.com/2008/05/19/business/media/19newshour.html?th=&adxnnl=1&e.

[46]From an interview, December 18, 2002.

[47]Quentin Schultze blog posting on February 8, 2008 at http://quentinschultze.blogspot.com/.

[48]Quentin J. Schultze, *Communicating for Life* (Grand Rapids: Baker Academic, 2000).

[49]Ibid., 127.

[50]Ibid.

[51]Ruben Navarrette, "PBS gets lesson in diversity," *The Indianapolis Star,* May 28, 2007, through www.indystar.com.

[52]See www.sourcewatch.org/index.php?title=Jacques_Ellul.

[53]Jacques Ellul, *Propaganda: The Formation of Men's Attitudes* (New York: Alfred A. Knopf, 1971).

[54]Vlogs are a video form of blogging.

[55]Merrill Brown, "Abandoning the News," *Carnegie Reporter,* 3, no. 2 (Spring 2005), http://www.carnegie.org/reporter/10/news/index.html.

[56]"AP Launches Mobile News Network," *Editor & Publisher* (May 5, 2008), http://www.editorandpublisher.com/eandp/news/article_display.jsp?vnu_content_id=1003798478.

[57]From http://propublica.org/full_mission.html.

Chapter 3: The Media Literacy Toolbox

[1]"Candidates Fight to Disprove Smears, Set Record Straight to Voters," *The News Hour,* PBS, June 30, 2008, http://www.pbs.org/newshour/topic/media/.

[2]See http://www.medialit.org/. According to CML's President, Tessa Jolls: It is the learning, practicing, and mastering of the Five Key Questions–*over time*–that lead to an adult understanding of how media are created and what their purposes are along with an informed ability to accept or reject both explicit and implicit messages. If democracy is to flourish in a global media culture, future citizens must have these fundamental skills.

[3]Canada has been a leader in media literacy. See some of the instructional philosophy at this site: http://www.medialit.org/reading_room/article338.html.

⁴The Raelian movement founded the Clonaid company, which claimed to have produced the first cloned baby, according to a BBC News report December 28, 2002. See http://news.bbc.co.uk/1/hi/health/2610795.stm. Hwang Woo Suk, the South Korean scientist, was denounced for falsifying his research evidence. See http://www.iht.com/articles/2006/01/11/news/clone.php.

⁵Tami Abdollah, "That 'new shower curtain smell' gives off toxic chemicals, study says," *Los Angeles Times,* June 13, 2008, http://www.latimes.com/features/health/medicine/la-me-showercurtain13-2008jun13,0,5417857.story.

⁶Joanne Kaufman, "Need Press? Repeat: 'Green,' 'Sex,' 'Cancer,' 'Secret,' 'Fat'," *The New York Times,* June 30, 2008, http://www.nytimes.com/2008/06/30/business/media/30toxic.html?th&emc=th.

⁷Ibid.

⁸*CML MediaLit Kit* (Malibu, Calif.: Center for Media Literacy), 11.

⁹Bob McCannon. "The language of persuasion," New Mexico Media Literacy Project, 2001, http://www.nmmlp.org.

¹⁰David Zucchino and Rick Loomis, "A final, respectful farewell," *Los Angeles Times,* reprinted in *The Indianapolis Star,* June 26, 2008, A3. The two reporters comment on the ban as being "haphazardly enforced and poorly understood, even among public affairs officers." One of these officers escorted the reporters to watch the ceremony, returning to them after conferring with another officer, to say they had to remain behind a security fence.

¹¹"Workers Remove 10 Commandments Monument," Associated Press story, August 27, 2003, http://www.beliefnet.com/story/131/story_13153.html.

¹²For an excellent discussion of hub symbols, see Joseph Webb, *Preaching and the Challenge of Pluralism* (St. Louis: Chalice Press, 1998), 47–61.

¹³Associated Press, "Clinton misspoke about '96 Bosnia trip," *USA Today,* March 25, 2008, http://www.usatoday.com/news/politics/election2008/2008-03-24-clinton-bosnia_N.htm.

¹⁴The rallies took place on August 24, 2003, and were covered by the city's print and electronic media.

¹⁵Erin Dostal, "Muslims to get floor sinks at airport by fall," *The Indianapolis Star,* April 4, 2008.

¹⁶David Bauder, "Blogs make spreading untruths easier," Associated Press story, January 30, 2007.

¹⁷Reaction to the story by Eli Saslow in the *Washington Post* on June 30, 2008, was reported the next day in the online version of Findley's local paper, *The Courier.* See http://www.thecourier.com/Issues/2008/Jul/01/ar_news_070108_story1.asp?d=070108_story1,2008,Jul,01&c=n.

¹⁸Jim Rutenberg, "Political Freelancers Use Web to Join the Attack," *The New York Times,* June 29, 2008, http://www.nytimes.com/2008/06/30/us/politics/30swift.html?pagewanted=2&th&emc=th.

¹⁹This excellent and thought-provoking article compares the U.S. model with that of Canada and other countries as it reports on the trial of a magazine in Canada for its piece that discussed Islam as threatening the values of the West. Adam Liptak, "Unlike Others, U.S. Defends Freedom to Offend in Speech," *The New York Times,* June 12, 2008, www.nytimes.com/2008/06/12/us/12hate.html?_=1&th=&emc=th&a dxnnix=12132.

²⁰Quote from the *Cophenhagen Post,* see http://blog.newspaperindex.com/2005/12/10.

²¹"Pfizer Cancels Dr. Jarvik Lipitor Commercial After Congressional Investigation," http://www.clevelandleader.com/node/4823.

²²Thom Hartmann, "What Would Machiavelli Do? The Big Lie Lives On," http://www.commondreams.org/views04/0826-02.htm: "German filmmaker Fritz Kippler, one of Goebbels' most effective propagandists, once said that two steps were necessary to promote a Big Lie so the majority of the people in a nation would believe it. The first was to reduce an issue to a simple black-and-white choice that

'even the most feebleminded could understand.' The second was to repeat the oversimplification over and over. If these two steps were followed, people would always come to believe the Big Lie."

[23]The article, written by McCain's campaign manager, chronicles the twisting of the facts about the McCains' adopting a child from Bangladesh into a story about McCain having an illegitimate black child. Richard H. Davis, "The anatomy of a smear campaign," *The Boston Globe,* March 21, 2004, http://www.boston.com/news/globe/editorial_opinion/oped/articles/2004/03/21/the_anatomy_of_a_smear_campaign/.

[24]Associated Press, "Former Classmates Say Virginia Tech Killer Was Picked on in High School," April 20, 2007, Foxnews.com, http://www.foxnews.com/story/0,2933,266921,00.html.

[25]Racist remarks made on-air and in public presentations dominated public discussion in 2007. Don Imus lost his job in broadcasting in April 2007. Previously, comedian Michael Richards' racist comment to a heckler was widely publicized, as was that of Indiana's Secretary of State Todd Rokita, who used a racist image during a speech.

[26]Eric Lichtblau, "Suit Challenges Constitutionality Of Powers in Antiterrorism Law," *The New York Times,* July 31, 2003, http://www.nytimes.com/2003/07/31/national/31PATR.html?th=&pagewanted=print&posi.

[27]Associated Press, "Israelis see Syria talks as a diversion from Olmert scandal," *International Herald Tribune,* May 22, 2008, http://www.iht.com/articles/ap/2008/05/22/africa/ME-GEN-Israel-Syria.php.

[28]See http://en.wikipedia.org/wiki/Enron; http://en.wikipedia.org/wiki/Subprime_mortgage_crisis.

[29]Amy Merrick, "Frustration Builds as Property Taxes Rise," *The Wall Street Journal Online,* December 19, 2007, http://www.realestatejournal.com/buysell/taxesandinsurance/20071219-merrick.html.

[30]Fred. B. Craddock, *As One Without Authority* (St. Louis: Chalice Press, 2001), 49. Craddock, ordained in the Christian Church (Disciples of Christ), is known for promoting inductive preaching.

[31]Augustine of Hippo, *On Christian Doctrine,* book 4, chapter 2, in *Select Library of Nicene and Post-Nicene Fathers,* ed. Philip Schaff (New York: Wm. B. Eerdmans, 1989), http://www.cartage.org.1b/en/themes/Book/Libr[a]ry/books/bibliographie/A/Augu/ChristianD.

[32]Jay Davis, "Beyond the Myth of Objectivity," *Media & Values* (Spring 1990).

[33]Adapted from Patricia Hynds, "Balance Bias With Critical Questions," *Media & Values* (Spring 1990): 2-3, available at http://www.medialit.org/ReadingRoom/Media&Values/Balance_Bias.html.

[34]Presentation at Spirit and Place 2002 conference in Indianapolis.

[35]From http://www.journalism.org. In 1999, The Project for Excellence in Journalism and Princeton Survey Research Associates produced a survey, funded by the Pew Charitable Trust, called *Framing the News: The Triggers, Frames and Messages in Newspaper Coverage.* The results were published on what is now the joint Web site of the Project for Excellence in Journalism and the Committee of Concerned Journalists. At this site, readers can view articles, book reviews, ethics discussions and statements, journalism tools, a daily briefing with current analysis, and a section devoted to education and training

[36]"Q&A: Flood Worries Spread in Illinois, Missouri," National Public Radio, June 20, 2008, http://www.npr.org/templates/story/story.php?storyId=91557702.

[37]United Press International, "Ban calls Zimbabwe Election Flawed," June 30, 2008, http://www.upi.com/Top_News/2008/06/30/Ban_calls_Zimbabwe_election_flawed/UPI-58861214841949/.

[38]UN News Centre, "UN Assembly condemns Holocaust denial by consensus; Iran disassociates itself ," January 26, 2007, http://www.un.org/apps/news/story.asp?NewsID=21355&Cr=holocaust&Cr1.

[39]Lloyd Dunkelberger, "Judge: Case built on 'speculation and conjecture,'" *Herald Tribune*, December 30, 2006, http://www.heraldtribune.com/apps/pbcs.dll/article?AID=/20061230/NEWS/612300599.

[40]"JASI to Celebrate 20 Years," *Inside Indiana Business* report, June 2, 2008, http://www.insideindianabusiness.com/newsitem.asp?id=29647.

[41]Nguyen Huy Vu, Associated Press, "Officials debate future of death penalty in Illinois," June 30, 2008, http://www.stltoday.com/stltoday/news/stories.nsf/illinoisnews/story/8180F089A121F2EA86257478000EB8A4?OpenDocument.

[42]David Broder, "Reality vs. the Mythmakers," *Washington Post*, June 1, 2008, http://www.washingtonpost.com/wp-dyn/content/article/2008/05/30/AR2008053002519.html.

[43]Cathryn Creno, Gannett News Service, "Product shrinkage eats into wallets," *The Indianapolis Star*, June 29, 2008, http://www.indystar.com/apps/pbcs.dll/article?AID=/20080629/BUSINESS/806290333.

[44]Francesca Jarosz, "Judge tosses law on adult materials," *The Indianapolis Star*, July 2, 2008, http://www.indystar.com/apps/pbcs.dll/article?AID=/20080702/LOCAL18/807020420.

[45]Jennifer Medina, "Students, Teachers and Parents Weigh in on State of the Schools," *The New York Times*, July 2, 2008, http://www.nytimes.com/2008/07/02/education/02survey.html.

[46]Peter S. Goodman, "Deepening Cycle of Job Loss Seen Lasting Into '09," *The New York Times*, July 2, 2008, http://www.nytimes.com/2008/07/02/business/02jobs.html?_r=1&hp&oref=slogin.

[47]"Holding health hostage, making millions wait," *The Indianapolis Star*, June 26, 2008, http://www.indystar.com/apps/pbcs.dll/article?AID=/20080626/OPINION08/806260310/1291/OPINION08.

[48]"Framing the News: The Triggers, Frames, and Messages in Newspaper Coverage," July 13, 1998, *http://www.journalism.org/node/445.*

[49]Whitney Smith, "Nurturing the Arts," *The Indianapolis Star*, June 29, 2008, http://www.indy.com/posts/9351.

[50]Project for Excellence in Journalism, "Changing Definitions of News," March 6, 1998, http://www.journalism.org.

[51]Greg Miller, "Climate change likely to trigger global destabilization, report says," *Los Angeles Times*, June 26, 2008, http://www.latimes.com/news/science/environment/la-na-intel26-2008jun26,0,6926278.story.

[52]Kevin Rector, "Watchdogs with Teeth," *American Journalism Review* (June/July 2008), http://www.ajr.org/Article.asp?id=4554.

[53]"Charles Woodson to hold charity wine event in Ann Arbor," *Detroit Free Press*, July 2, 2008, http://www.freep.com/apps/pbcs.dll/article?AID=/20080702/SPORTS06/307020004.

[54]Pew Research Center Publications, "The U.S. Religious Landscape Survey Reveals a Fluid and Diverse Pattern of Faith," February 25, 2008, http://pewresearch.org/pubs/743/united-states-religion.

[55]John Heilprin, Associated Press, "AP interview: Iran envoy dismisses attack threat," WTOP news.com, July 2, 2008, http://www.wtopnews.com/?nid=104&pid=0&sid=1432978&page=2.

[56]The newspapers included *The New York Times, Washington Post, Los Angeles Times, Atlanta Journal Constitution, Idaho Statesman, Rocky Mountain News,* and *Minneapolis Star-Tribune.*

[57]George Will, "Smart and foreign-born? Sorry to see you go," *The Indianapolis Star,* June 26, 2008, http://www.indystar.com/apps/pbcs.dll/article?AID=/20080626/OPINION12/806260311/1002/OPINION.

[58]Dana Knight, "Summer jobs meltdown," *The Indianapolis Star*, June 29, 2008, http://www.indystar.com/apps/pbcs.dll/article?AID=/20080629/BUSINESS/806290325.

[59]Samantha Henry, Associated Press, "Restaurateur's specialty: U.S.-North Korea relations," *The Indianapolis Star*, June 28, 2008, http://www.washingtonpost.com/wp-dyn/content/article/2008/06/28/AR2008062800818.html?sub=AR.

[60]Eugene White and David Godsted, "The power of literacy," *The Indianapolis Star*, June 29, 2008, http://www.indystar.com/apps/pbcs.dll/article?AID=2008806290347.

[61]Danny Hakim and William K. Rashbaum, "Spitzer is Linked to Prostitution Ring," *The New York Times*, March 10, 2008, http://www.nytimes.com/2008/03/10/nyregion/10cnd-spitzer.html.

[62]Timothy Sullivan, Associated Press, "The nightmares remain," News24.com, http://www.news24.com/News24/World/News/0,,2-10-1462_2323514,00.html.

[63]For a biography and excellent discussion of his contributions to education, see this comprehensive online article: http://www3.nl.edu/academics/cas/ace/resources/paulofreire.cfm.

Chapter 4: Preacher as Mediator of the News and the Good News

[1]Ted Evanoff et al, "Putting up a fight," *The Indianapolis Star,* June 10, 2008, A1.

[2]Samuel Proctor, *Preaching about Crisis in the Community* (Philadelphia: The Westminster Press, 1988), 79.

[3]Joseph Jeter, *Crisis Preaching: Personal and Public* (Nashville: Abingdon Press, 1998), 11, 22.

[4]Fred B. Craddock, *Preaching* (Nashville: Abingdon Press, 1985), 93–98.

[5]Luke 2:41–52

[6]Ed Mitchell, "Daily Scripture Reflections from St. Monica Parish," Indianapolis, July 6, 2007.

[7]The Myers & Briggs Foundation, http://www.myersbriggs.org/my-mbti-personality-type/mbti-basics/ .

[8]Joseph R. Jeter, Jr., and Ronald J. Allen, *One Gospel, Many Ears: Preaching for Different Listeners in the Congregation* (St. Louis: Chalice Press, 2002).

[9]James W. Fowler, *Stages of Faith* (New York: HarperCollins, 1995).

[10]From http://www.indystar.com/apps/pbcs.dll/article?AID=/20080530/BUSINESS/80530042.

[11]Burton Z. Cooper and John S. McClure, *Claiming Theology in the Pulpit* (Louisville: Westminster John Knox Press, 2003), 46–55.

[12]From http://www.nytimes.com/2006/03/19/weekinreview/19swarns.html.

[13]From http://www.cnn.com/2007/US/04/24/Dobbs.April25/index.html.

[14]"Fear and Loathing in Prime Time: Immigration Myths and Cable News," http://mediamattersaction.org.

[15]G. Bromley Oxnam, *Preaching and Social Crisis* (New York: Abingdon Press, 1933).

[16]Proctor, *Preaching about Crisis.*

[17]See http://www.geisheker.com/repetition.htm.

[18]See www.juneteenth.com, www.lirs.org, www.childrensdefensefund.org/childrens_sabbaths.

[19]For a discussion of preaching during the feasts and seasons of the liturgical year, as well as for sacramental rites, see James Wallace, *Preaching to the Hungers of the Heart: Preaching on the Feasts and Within the Rites* (Collegeville, Minn.: Liturgical Press, 2002).

[20]Ronald Rohlheiser, *The Holy Longing: The Search for a Christian Spirituality* (New York: Doubleday, 1999), 147.

[21]Ibid.

[22]Justo L. and Catherine González, *Liberation Preaching: the Pulpit and the Oppressed* (Nashville: Abingdon Press, 1980), 106–7.

[23]Mary Gail Frawley-O'Dea, "Commentary: Papal visit a 'both/and' moment in sex abuse crisis," *National Catholic Reporter*, May 16, 2008, http://ncronline3.org/drupal/?q=print/983.

[24]Ibid.

[25]Ibid.

[26]Nicholas D. Kristof, "Inviting All Democrats," *The New York Times,* January 14, 2004.

[27]See http://globalexchange.org/campaigns/fairtrade/coffee/retailers.html.

[28]Jane Mary Trau, *The Co-Existence of God and Evil*, American University Studies, series 5, Philosophy, vol. 101 (New York: Peter Lang, 1991), 19.

[29]J. Philip Wogamon, *Speaking the Truth in Love: Prophetic Preaching to a Broken World* (Louisville: Westminster John Knox Press, 1998), 52.

[30]Roland Q. Leavell, *Prophetic Preaching, Then and Now* (Grand Rapids, Mich.: Baker Book House, 1963), 31.

[31]Ibid.

[32]Bill Kovach and Tom Rosenstiel, *The Elements of Journalism* (New York: Three Rivers Press, 2001), 129. The actual quote reprinted from *Bartlett's Quotations* came from Finley Peter Dunne, a Chicago journalist and humorist, who was talking about the role of journalist as a watchdog in society. Dunne's words are spoken by a fictional character, Mr. Dooley: "The newspaper does everything for us. It runs the police force and the banks, commands the militia, controls the legislature, baptizes the young, marries the foolish, comforts the afflicted and afflicts the comfortable, buries the dead, and roasts them afterward."

[33]The International Society for Traumatic Stress Studies post 9/11, "ISTSS Members, Mental Health Professionals and Teachers,' www.istss.org.

[34]Jessica Hamblen, "Terrorist Attacks and Children: A National Center for PTSD Fact Sheet," Department of Veterans Affairs, http://www.ncptsd.org/facts/disasters/fs_helping_survivors.html. Based on a study conducted by Pfefferbaum and Associates in 1999–2000.

[35]"What are the symptoms of PTSD?" PTSD Alliance, http://www.ptsdalliance.org/about_symp.html.

[36]Charles R. Figley, "The Columbia Space Shuttle Tragedy: An Essay," February 1, 2003, http://www.giftfromwithin.org/html/columbia/html.

[37]Ibid.

[38]David Fleer and Dave Bland, eds., *Preaching Autobiography: Connecting the World of the Preacher and the World of the Text* (Abilene, Texas: ACU Press, 2001), 247.

[39]Ralph L. Underwood, *Pastoral Care and the Means of Grace* (Minneapolis: Augsburg Fortress, 1993), 47.

[40]Eric Reed, "Special: When the News Intrudes: What do you say from the pulpit about national crises and tragedies?" *Preaching Today* (March 13, 2003): Dale Clem recounts their ordeal in *Winds of Fury, Circles of Grace: Life After the Palm Sunday Tornadoes* (Nashville, Abingdon Press, 1997). See a local blogger's account at http://keeepinthefaith.blogspot.com/2006_04_01_archive.html.

[41]Ronald J. Sider and Michael A. King, *Preaching About Life in a Threatening World* (Philadelphia: Westminster Press, 1987), 114.

[42]Philip Gulley and James Mulholland, *If Grace Is True: Why God Will Save Every Person* (New York: HarperCollins, 2003).

[43]Robert Waznak, "Preaching Faith in the Midst of Tragedy," *America* (October 8, 2001).

[44]Rev. Michael Mooty, excerpt from a letter to the congregation of Central Christian Church, Lexington, Kentucky, following the Virginia Tech massacre of students and faculty on April 16, 2007.

Chapter 5: What Preachers Can Learn from Journalists

[1]From a Larry King Live tribute program to the late Tim Russert on June 13, 2008, http://transcripts.cnn.com/TRANSCRIPTS/0806/13/lkl.01.html.

[2]See http://www.cnn.com/2008/US/06/15/russert.sunday/.

[3]For a discussion of the purposes of journalism, see Bill Kovach and Tom Rosenstiel, *The Elements of Journalism* (New York: Three Rivers Press, 2001), chapter 1.

[4]See http://www.nytimes.com/ref/opinion/KRISTOF-BIO.html?pagewanted=print, April 16, 2006.

[5]See http://pbs.org/newshour/bb/media/jan-june06/kristof_4-20.html.

⁶Ibid.

⁷See www.childrensdefense.org.

⁸Congress passed S2499 in December 2007, which extends SCHIP through March 2009 only to maintain the 2007 levels of support. For additional information, see The State Children's Health Insurance Program (SCHIP), http://www.results. org/website/article.asp?id=1561.

⁹See http://select.nytimes.com/2007/07/30/opinion/30krugman. html?th=&emc=th&pagewanted.

¹⁰Audio is available at Web site for Kansas Public Radio broadcast of "Paul Krugman, America's Health Care Crisis," May 7, 2007, http://kansaspublicradio. org/newsstory.php?itemID=3289).

¹¹Fred B. Craddock, *As One Without Authority* (St. Louis: Chalice Press, 2001), 119.

¹²See http://select.nytimes.com/2007/09/12/opinion/12friedman.html?th=& adxnnl=1&emc=th&.

¹³Gregory Rodriquez, *Mongrels, Bastards, Orphans, and Vagabonds: Mexican Immigration and the Future of Race in America* (New York: Random House, 2007).

¹⁴Gregory Rodriguez, "Doubts of the faithful," *Los Angeles Times*, September 10, 2007, A17.

¹⁵Leonard Pitts, "I know he's out there – somewhere," *Miami Herald*, September 2, 2007. http://www.asne.org/index.cfm?ID=6830#somewhere.

¹⁶Leonard Pitts, "Message to a young man in detention," *Miami Herald*, August 26, 2007.

¹⁷Bob Herbert, "The Man in the Room," New York Times, June 17, 2008, http://www. nytimes.com/2008/06/17/opinion/17herbert.html?th=&emc=th&pagewanted=p.

¹⁸Jamie Passaro, "Barbara Ehrenreich Leads 'Writing About' Workshop," *Flash* 15, no. 2 at http://flash.uoregon.edu/U00/ehrenreich.html.

¹⁹Barbara Ehrenreich, "Smashing Capitalism," *The Nation* (Aug. 20, 2007), http://www.thenation.com/docprint.mhtml?i=20070827&s=ehrenreich.

²⁰Peggy Noonan, "Spouse Rules," *The Wall Street Journal*, Aug. 3, 2007, http:// www.peggynoonan.com/article.php?article=375.

²¹See this nonpolitical site to check data: www.factcheck.org.

²²"Quindlen: America Needs its Newcomers," *Newsweek* magazine, August 20–27, 2008 at http://www.newsweek.com/id/32273.

²³Hazelton's restrictive local laws, which barred undocumented immigrants from employment and rental housing, were struck down in Federal Court in 2007, while Riverside rescinded its ordinances fearing a costly court battle.

Chapter 6: Behind the Scenes of the First "Preaching When the News Disturbs" Workshop

¹See http://www.cnn.com/2004/US/02/02/superbowl.jackson/.

²Networks took proposed fines for indecency seriously and delayed broadcasts to catch inappropriate material. CBS lost an appeal to avoid payment of a $550,000 fine for the Super Bowl clothing issue in 2004. See "FCC Firm on Super Bowl Fine," CBS News, Feb. 23, 2006, http://www.cbsnews.com/stories/2006/02/23/entertainment/ main1340839.shtml. After further discussion in Congress the fine was overturned. See Peter Kaplan, "Court overturns CBS fine over Janet Jackson flash," July 21, 2008, http://uk.reuters.com/article/UKNews1/idUKN2140410720080721.

³David Chazan, "Who are the Raelians?" BBC News, http://news.bbc.co.uk/1/ hi/health/2610795.stm.

⁴This claim was revealed as fraudulent in 2005. See Anthony Faiola and Rick Weiss, "South Korean Panel Debunks Scientist's Stem Cell Claims," *Washington Post Foreign Service*, January 10, 2006, AO9, at http://www.washingtonpost.com/wp-dyn/ content/article/2006/01/09/AR2006010901943.html.

[5]Gardiner Harris, "Student, 19, in Trial of New Antidepressant Commits Suicide," *The New York Times,* February 12, 2004, http://query.nytimes.com/gst/fullpage.html? res=9C03E5D8133AF931A25751C0A9629C8B63.

[6]See http://www.partnersinpreaching.org/who.html.

Appendix A: The Roots of Today's Disturbing News and the Implications for Preaching

[1]Catholic News Agency, "Ex-priest says silencing of Father Sobrino will reanimate liberation theology in Latin America," http://www.catholicnewsagency.com/new.php?n=8887, March 16, 2007.

[2]Friction resulted between the local leadership of liberation theology movements and the central seat of Roman Catholic authority in the Vatican. As Prefect of the Congregation for the Doctrine of the Faith from 1981, Cardinal Ratzinger, now Pope Benedict XVI, condemned the work of widely-known liberation theologians Peruvian Gustavo Gutiérrez, Brazilian Leonardo Boff, and recently, Spaniard Jon Sobrino.

[3]Alfred Hennelly, S.J., *Liberation Theologies: The Global Pursuit of Justice* (Mystic, Conn.:Twenty-third Publications, 1995), 17.

[4]Thomas L. Schubeck, S.J. *Liberation Ethics: Sources, Models, and Norms* (Minneapolis: Augsburg Fortress, 1993).

[5]Larry Rohter, "As Pope Heads to Brazil, a Rival Theology Persists," *The New York Times,* May 7, 2007, http://www.nytimes.com/2007/05/07/world/americas/07theology.html?_r=1&hp=&pagewa.

[6]Hennelly, *Liberation Theologies,* 170.

[7]Peter S. Goodman, Washington Post Foreign Service, "China Invests Heavily in Sudan's Oil Industry, Beijing Supplies Arms Used on Villagers," *Washington Post,* Dec. 23, 2004, A01, http://www.washingtonpost.com/wp-dyn/articles/A21143-2004Dec22.html.

[8]Maureen Koch, "The Emergence of Sharia Law," *Online Newshour,* Public Broadcasting Service, July 2003. Although Christians are not subject to Sharia law, its use in the predominantly Muslim northern states has created an atmosphere of unease and intimidation between religious groups, causing tensions that have often led to violence. See http://www.pbs.org/newshour/bb/africa/nigeria/sharia_law.html.

[9]See Deane William Ferm's article, "Outlining Rice-Roots Theology," at http://www.religion-online.org/showarticle.asp?title=1367.

[10]One of the many Asian manifestations of religious opposition to oppression developed from the Korean experience of liberating oppressed people, the "Minjung," from "han," a state of powerful unresolved pain due to injustice derived from "classism, racism, sexism, colonialism, neo-colonialism, and cultural imperialism."

[11]Among theologians who have valued the contributions of non-Christian religions are Anthony De Mello, Thomas Merton, Raimundo Pannikar, and Bede Griffith.

[12]Hennelly, *Liberation Theologies,* 223.

[13]Unfortunately, these enlightened theologians who have spent many years in Asia have found their writings criticized by Vatican theologians. In 2000, the Vatican issued a document that claimed the "Roman Catholic Church was the only instrument for the salvation of all humanity." "Declaration Dominus Iesus" ("On the Unicity and Salvific Universality of Jesus Christ and the Church") states that non-Christian religions are gravely deficient and non-Catholic Christian bodies are defective. In July 2007, the Vatican reiterated these statements.

[14]"Summary of Key Findings, The U.S. Religious Landscape Survey, 2007," http://religions.pewforum.org/reports.

[15]James H. Cone, *God of the Oppressed,* rev. ed. (Maryknoll, N.Y.: Orbis Books, 1997,) ix.

[16]Jason Byassee, "A Visit to Chicago's Trinity UCC Africentric Church," *Christian Century* (May 29, 2007): 22. Quote is from *Blow the Trumpet in Zion* (Minneapolis:

Fortress Press, 2005). Dr. Wright was one of the editors, along with Iva Carruthers and Frederick D. Haynes III.

[17]Foon Rhee, "Obama disavows Rev. Wright," *The Boston Globe*, April 29, 2008, http://www.boston.com/news/politics/politicalintelligence/2008/04/obama_disavows.html.

[18]I found chapters 5 and 6 of Richard Cleaver's book *Know My Name: A Gay Liberation Theology* (Louisville: Westminster John Knox Press, 1995) to be especially poignant as they spoke to liturgical exclusion.

[19]See "Presbyterians Vote to Drop Ban on Gay Ordination," http://seattlest.com/2008/06/28/presbyterians_vote_to_drop_ban_on_g.php.

[20]Hennelly, *Liberation Theologies*, 275.

[21]Quoted in Sallie McFague's article in Charles Birch, William Eakin, and Jay McDaniel, eds., *Liberating Life: Contemporary Approaches to Ecological Theology* (Maryknoll, N.Y.: Orbis Books, 1990), 201–27.

[22]Ibid., 278–79. Each of these twelve statements could occupy scientists, theologians, and philosophers for many lifetimes. The final statement is the departure for doing ecotheology: "The main human task of the immediate future is to assist in activating the intercommunion of all the living and non-living components of the Earth community in what can be considered the emerging ecological period of Earth development."

[23]Mary Catherine Hilkert, *Naming Grace: Preaching and the Sacramental Imagination* (New York: Continuum, 1997), 42.

[24]For an excellent overview of this period of expansion and imperialism see http://www.microworks.net/pacific/road_to_war/pr_us_to1898.htm.

[25]See excellent article "National Framework for Globalization" at http://www.itcilo.it/english/actrav/telearn/global/ilo/frame/national.htm.

[26]For excellent articles describing ethnicity and migration in Sudan, see the following online articles: http://www.geocities.com/forsudan/poulation.html http://freedomhouse.org/modules/mod_call_dsp_country-fiw.cfm?year=2007& country=7277, and http://www.refugeesinternational.org/content/article/detail/ 8826/.

[27]See Thomas L. Friedman's books *The Lexus and the Olive Tree* (New York: Anchor, 2000) and *The World Is Flat*, rev. ed. (New York: Farrar, Straus, and Giroux, 2006), to learn more about globalization in the twenty-first-century context.

[28]See http://www.supremecourtus.gov/opinions/06pdf/05-1074.pdf. Even in the United States, the Supreme Court upholds gender pay disparity on a technicality.

[29]For information about globalization and its effects on the poor, see http://www.globalpolicy.org/globaliz/index.htm.

[30]See discussion in chapter 3.

[31]Joerg Rieger. *God and the Excluded: Visions and Blindspots in Contemporary Theology* (Minneapolis: Fortress Press, 2001), x.

[32]Gustavo Gutiérrez. *The God of Life*, trans. Matthew J. O'Connell (New York: Orbis Books, 1991).

[33]See list of publications at http://www.eatwot.org/.

[34]Rev. Carmelo Álvarez serves as a missionary affiliate appointed by the Common Global Ministries Board of the Christian Church (Disciples of Christ) and the United Church of Christ to serve with the Latin American Evangelical Pentecostal Commission (CEPLA) and the Evangelical Pentecostal Union of Venezuela (UEPV) based in Chicago. He serves as program consultant and visiting professor for the Latin American Pentecostal Commission (CEPLA) and the Evangelical Pentecostal Union of Venezuela (UEPV). His seven practices for freeing the oppressed were articulated at Christian Theological Seminary in October 2002 during Rev. Alvarez's Liberation Theology course.

[35]United States Catholic Conference, *Renewing the Earth: An Invitation to Reflection and Action on Environment in Light of Social Teaching* (Washington D.C., 1991), 13.

[36]Eric Lipton and David Barboza "Unsafe Chinese Toys Cause Alarm," *International Herald Tribune*, June 18, 2007, http://www.iht.com/articles/2007/06/18/

business/toys.php; Katie Bird, "Unsafe Chinese cosmetics still a worry, says EU official," June 11, 2008, CosmeticsDesign.com, http://www.cosmeticsdesign.com/news/ng.asp?id=85847-china-toxic-skin-care.

[37]For a brief history of Islamist terrorism, see "The Rise and Decline of Al Qaeda," the July 9, 2003, statement of Rohan Gunaratna to the National Commission on Terrorist Attacks, available on the commission's Web site: http://www.9-11commission.gov/hearings/hearing3/witness_gunaratna.htm.

[38]For a concise chronological overview, see John Moore, "The Evolution of Islamic Terrorism: An Overview," at http://www.pbs.org/wgbh/pages/frontline/shows/target/etc/modern.html.

[39]"Panel of Christians Speaks Out on War With Iraq," *CNN Larry King Live,* March 11, 2003. Transcript available at http://edition.cnn.com/TRANSCRIPTS/0303/11/1kl.00.html.

[40]Mark O'Keefe's piece from Religion News Service pointed out that both the Southern Baptist Convention and Rev. Franklin Graham's Samaritan's Purse are two evangelical groups bringing aid, as well as the Gospel, to Iraq in the aftermath of war. The heads of both organizations have spoken for the record about their understanding of Islam. Graham was quoted in December 2001 as saying that Islam is "a very evil and wicked religion," and in a book published in 2002, "The God of Islam is not the God of the Christian faith." Rev. Jerry Vines, who is a former president of the Southern Baptist Convention, addressed delegates to the 2002 convention in St. Louis, saying, "And I will tell you Allah is not Jehovah, either. Jehovah's not going to turn you into a terrorist." Reporting on the May 7, 2003, meeting held by the National Association of Evangelicals, Laurie Goodstein of *The New York Times* quoted leaders who denounced the anti-Islam rhetoric of Graham and others. For example, Dr. Clive Calver said: "It's very dangerous to build more barriers when we're supposed to be following the one who pulled the barriers down." Referring to Graham's words as "circulating widely," he went on to say: "It's used to indict all Americans and used to indict all Christians. It obviously puts lives and livelihoods of people overseas at risk."

[41]"PBS Provides Comprehensive 9/11 Programming Across Iconic Series," lists documentaries through 2006. See http://www.pbs.org/aboutpbs/news/20060821_PBS9-11.html.

[42]The issue included a report on America's Muslims and an excellent commentary "What America and Islam Share," by Imam Feisal Abdul Rauf and Daisy Khan, that compares the values inherent in both the faith and nation. Online, see http://today.msnbc.msn.com/id/19889242/site/newsweek/.

[43]Barbara Bradley Hagerty, "Imam Serves as Islam's Face to Community," *All Things Considered,* National Public Radio, August 6, 2007. See http://www.npr.org/templates/story/story.php?storyId=12532168.

[44]Samir Amin, "Political Islam"(2001), available at www.loompanics.com/Articles/PoliticalIslam.html.

[45]Khaled Abou El Fadl. "Islam and the Theology of Power," *Middle East Report* 221 (Winter 2001): 4–5, http://www.merip.org/mer/mer221/221_abu_el_fadl.html.

[46]Ibid, 5.

[47]Teresa Watanabe, "American Muslims Debate Large Donation by Saudi Prince," *Los Angeles Times,* December 1, 2002, reprinted at http://www.cantonrep.com/index.php?Category=23&ID=74020&r=0.

[48]Hillel Gl. Fradkin, "Radical Islam and Global Terrorism: What is it and What are its Causes?" September 26, 2002, at https://eppc.org/publications/task.execute/pub_byauthor_list.asp51.

[49]For excellent background pieces, see Richard N. Haass, "The New Middle East," *Foreign Affairs* (Nov. 1, 2006) and http://www.globalissues.org/geopolitics/MiddleEast.asp.

[50]Ibid. See also John Moore, "The Evolution of Islamic Terrorism, an Overview, *Frontline,* Public Broadcasting Service, http://www.pbs.org/wgbh/pages/frontline/shows/target/etc/modern.html.

[51]See also Mark Levine, "Muslim Responses to Globalization," International Institute for the Study of Islam in the Modern World newsletter July 10, 2002,http://www.isim.nl/files/newsl_10.pdf. According to Mark Levine, in 2002, 30 percent of Muslim immigrants were unemployed.

[52]Ibid. See also http://edition.cnn.com/2007/WORLD/europe/01/17/warwithin.amanpour/index.html. Christine Amanpour's documentary for CNN *The War Within* provided insight into a growing sector of second generation Islamist immigrants and their serious challenges in European countries.

[53]See Francis Fukuyama, Identity and Migration, Prospect Magazine 131 (February 2007), http://www.prospect-magazine.co.uk/printarticle.php?id=8239.

[54]Ibid.

[55]Ibid.

Appendix B: "Lament and Remember"

[1]RAND Center for Military Health Policy Research, April 18, 2008, http://rand.org/pubs/monographs/2008/RAND_MG720.pdf.